Willa Cather and
the Fairy Tale

Studies in Modern Literature, No. 97

Willa Cather and the Fairy Tale

by
Marilyn Berg Callander

UMI Research Press

Ann Arbor / London

Produced and distributed by
UMI Research Press
an imprint of
University Microfilms Inc.
Ann Arbor, Michigan 48106

Library of Congress Cataloging in Publication Data

Callander, Marilyn Berg, 1933-
   Willa Cather and the fairy tale.
   (Studies in modern literature ; no. 97)
   Bibliography: p.
   Includes index.
   1. Cather, Willa, 1873-1947—Knowledge—Folklore,
mythology. 2. Fairy tales—History and criticism.
3. Folklore in literature. I. Title. II. Series.
PS3505.A87Z59   1988   813'.52   88-27775
ISBN 0-8357-1929-4 (alk. paper)

British Library CIP data is available.

. . . for my father . . .

The speaker in this case
is a middle-aged witch, me—
tangled on my two great arms,
my face in a book
and my mouth wide,
ready to tell you a story or two.
I have come to remind you,
all of you:
Alice, Samuel, Kurt, Eleanor,
Jane, Brian, Maryel,
All of you draw near.
Alice,
at fifty-six do you remember?
Do you remember when you
were read to as a child?

From Anne Sexton's *Transformations*

Contents

Acknowledgments

Willa Cather said while she was still a young newspaper woman, "Surely we all know that the books we read when we were children shaped our lives; at least they shaped our imaginings, and it is with our imaginings that we live." Little did she know at the time how scholars would probe for the source of her own imaginings in the great literature she was yet to write.

I came to Cather as a college student, when the professor who changed the course of my life told me that *Death Comes for the Archbishop* was one of the great American novels. In 1955, that was a brave and original statement. But my own instincts agreed, and led me into *My Ántonia* and *Shadows on the Rock*. Not until graduate school, however, did I address Cather's fiction seriously. While taking a course in Willa Cather's work taught brilliantly by Merrill Skaggs at Drew University, fairy-tale lights began to flash in my head. My professors and colleagues wearied of hearing me say, "But can't you see? It's all a fairy tale." Of course, what was happening was that my own imaginings were at work; those stories I had read and loved as a child, which had helped to shape my vision of reality, were connecting in an exciting way with a writer whose work I had read and loved for most of my adult life.

And so firstly, I should be thankful for a family environment in which books were abundantly provided and reading nurtured, for growing up in a family who believed that pleasure lies in stories, and that along with the pleasure comes some truth and wisdom as well. Next I am thankful to Belle Matheson at Beaver College, and to Merrill Skaggs at Drew University, who believed in story as much as my own family, but who added a richly intellectual dimension to the pleasure.

I could never had made it through graduate school to the completion of this book, orchestrating a family at the same time, without real friends. Merrill remains ever the best. Barbara Caspersen and Jo Ann Middleton are Cather scholars who are always ready to escape with me into her language. Without Barbara, I would never have a sharpened pencil. Wajuppa Tossa and I talked far into the nights about fairy tales in Thailand, a living example of the continuous cross-cultural nourishment of people and tales.

A friend gave me one of Willa Cather's rare letters before I started this book. Cather writes to a fan in the letter that she can always tell when fans who write her have really gotten something out of her books, and when they merely think they have. Both the letter and the gift have inspired and sustained me.

My thanks to Professor Jacqueline Berke and Professor Janet Burstein for their always astute advice; to the infinitely patient research staff at the Drew University library; to my sister Susan, who came through at the last moment with details essential for meeting the publisher's deadline; to my children, who learned to live with tasks undone while I tried to keep the impossible balance between mother and scholar; and to my husband Bob for his forbearance and ever-increasing flexibility.

Introduction

In a 1982 article on Willa Cather, Bernice Slote states that Cather scholarship has been handicapped by "the neglect of clues and allusions within the work that in T. S. Eliot's *The Waste Land* (to give only one example) would have drawn forth tomes of analysis" (211). Cather uses such allusions, sometimes directly and sometimes indirectly, to prod her readers to notice "other dimensions of the world created" (213), while at the same time obscuring her clues with a deceptively simple style.[1]

Recent scholars have addressed themselves to Cather's specific references and allusions to American and European literature, the classics, Shakespeare, the Bible, and works of music, painting, and sculpture.[2] In all cases Cather's references within her texts are not incidental, but illuminate her novels in significant ways.

Yet to my knowledge, no one has to date addressed seriously Cather's many allusions and specific references to fairy tales. The Appendix at the end of this book listing some of Cather's references to fairy tales as well as to legends and fables, which are closely related forms, proves the extent to which these forms were a part of her thought processes throughout her writing career. I believe that understanding how and why she uses fairy tales is crucial to the understanding of Willa Cather's work.

As Aldo Celli points out, the archetypal dimension is strongly present in Cather's novels, revealing "a fable-like dimension" beneath. Using *O Pioneers!* as an example, Celli notes the presence of "the 'goddess-mother'; the despotic queen; the good, wise old man; the wandering knight; the bad brothers; the prince charming; the woman of fate; the victim of love" (*Art* 115). Celli has listed here some classic fairy-tale motifs; he fails to note Cather's allusions to specific fairy tales in the text of *O Pioneers!*,[3] and to make a connection between motifs and tales in Cather's work. Celli continues: "Like *fables* [my emphasis], Willa Cather's tales and novels are based on essential situations. . . . Like the *folktale* [my emphasis], Willa Cather's novels have the recurrent process of elaborating common material in a multidimensional context" (*Art* 115). Celli is astute in drawing our attention to this dimension in Cather's work. Focusing more specifically on this dimension, however, my chief concern here is not with folk-fairy tales[4] as part of the "collective unconscious," with the Jungian archetypal patterns that are so clearly present in Cather's fiction. Rather, my interest is in her conscious use of these forms.[5]

In an early newspaper article Cather writes, "Surely we all know that the books we read when we were children shaped our lives; at least they shaped our imaginings, and it is with our imaginings that we live" (*WP* 852). Drs. P. Knudson and C. Knudson, Fulbright scholars at the University of London, are currently studying Renaissance documents in an attempt to determine how humans learn to imagine.[6] Their theory is that since Elizabethan children were educated through the study of fables, their imaginations were therefore more richly metaphorical: the result of such an education was an era unsurpassed in human history in metaphorical richness. A projection of this fascinating theory is that any child raised on similar literature—on fables, legends, fairy tales, and the like—would not only have these images ingrained in the psyche, but would have a richer metaphorical imagination as well.

Reliable sources prove that Cather's imaginings were shaped by myth: her childhood reading was steeped in myth, and she read Grimms' *Fairy Tales, The Arabian Nights,* and Germanic-Norse folklore (*KA* 36). Cather loved Shakespeare all her life, and allusions to his work are liberally scattered throughout her own. Cather loved opera from her first exposure to it as a young adult, and allusions to opera abound in her work. And it is no coincidence that both Shakespeare and opera draw heavily from fairy tales. Henry James was Cather's most influential literary model, and James draws upon fairy tale even more extensively than Willa Cather.[7]

Biographers report that Cather enjoyed inventing tales for her younger brothers when they were children, and many of these tales, now available in *Collected Short Fiction,* are laced with fairy-tale conventions. Willa Cather once wrote a fairy tale of her own, "The Princess Baladina—Her Adventure," published in Pittsburgh's *Home Monthly* in 1896, under the pseudonym Charles Douglass. She never again employed the form so blatantly, and probably included this story on her list of those early pieces she wished could be lost forever; nonetheless, "Princess" is a droll and charming story which shows how thoroughly familiar Cather was with all aspects of fairy tale. Perhaps, too, it shows how much she delighted in the form.

Even in this very early piece, Cather plays with and challenges convention, as she was to do with all conventions throughout her life. Her story is full of the fairy-tale trappings—a golden-haired princess, a fairy godmother, a miller's son, a wizard, and a golden ball. Her princess, instead of being docile and submissive, scratches and bites the nurse who combs her golden hair, and is tempted to cut it off except that if a prince "should happen to come that way it would be awkward not to have any golden hair" (*SF* 568). Cather's princess is in search of her fairy tale; she runs away to find her prince, who, when she locates him, is too busy with the royal hunt to bother with a princess. "Princess Baladina," written just short of 100 years ago, sounds remarkably like the current prolific output of feminist fairy tales, in which princesses flaunt convention by insisting upon ruling kingdoms and driving trucks. Underlying Cather's fairy tale is her own enchantment with the form as well as her awareness that the rigidly stereotypic gender roles upon which fairy tale insists are unnatural and potentially destructive. The legacy they provide is contradictory: she must have admired the elegance of their form and style, the richness of their symbols and metaphors, while at the same time abhorring the lessons they teach for behavior, particularly female behavior.

Fairy-tale allusions run throughout Cather's fiction and produce different effects. Sometimes her characters have a kind of fairy-tale vision of reality— they build their understanding around fairy tales, with the resulting impairment in vision. Imogen in "Flavia and Her Artists," and Douglass in "The Treasure of Far Island" thus become forerunners in this respect of Jim Burden and Nellie Birdseye. Sometimes she uses motifs and figures; her princesses range from Thea to Cécile, her princes from Niel Herbert to Oswald Henshawe. Fairy-tale imagery, consciously and unconsciously, is a part of many stories and novels. Right through to one of her last stories, "The Old Beauty," fairy-tale elements embroider the fabric of Cather's work.

Fairy tales are Willa Cather's primary symbol of romance, woven through her works like a musical theme and variations. And this romance, whether it be romantic love, as in *The Song of the Lark* and *My Mortal Enemy;* an idyllic childhood, as in *My Ántonia;* or a heroic past, as in *Death Comes for the Archbishop* and *Shadows on the Rock,* is as much an illusion as a fairy tale. Jim Burden reminds himself that the "pale, cold light of the winter sunset did not beautify—it was like the light of truth itself" (173). The wind's bitter song says to him, "This is reality, whether you like it or not. All those frivolities of summer, the light and shadow, the living mask of green that trembled over everything, they were lies, and this is what was underneath. This is the truth" (173). Conversely, the closing words of Thea's favorite fairy tale are, "And it was Summer, Beautiful Summer!" (22). Fairy tales, like summer, represent illusion in Willa Cather's canon, superimposed upon winter's "reality."

Like a musical theme, too, fairy tale often disappears entirely, and then resurfaces. There are literally no allusions to fairy tale in some of the novels and stories. In *Alexander's Bridge,* Cather's first novel, there are two references to fairy tale, which have little bearing on the interpretation of the novel.[8] There are no allusions in *A Lost Lady:* although Niel Herbert is clearly one of Cather's romantics, his vision of the world is probably linked, as scholars have noted, to medieval courtly love rather than to fairy tale. Godfrey St. Peter, too, is one of Cather's romantics, but there are no allusions to fairy tale in *The Professor's House,* just as there are none of significance in *Lucy Gayheart* nor in *Sapphira and the Slave Girl.* Conversely, *The Song of the Lark, My Ántonia, My Mortal Enemy, Death Comes for the Archbishop,* and *Shadows on the Rock* are brimming with fairy-tale elements, as this study demonstrates. One of the most convincing aspects of the study is the fact that fairy tale is so clearly present in some of the novels and stories, and so conspicuously absent in others.

Many of Cather's critics mention the nostalgia for the past, especially childhood, which she expresses in her fiction. In *The Song of the Lark* she says that "art is only a way of remembering youth" (460). Given this information, one can easily see why she makes use of folk-fairy tales, which are the heart of children's stories, the finest representations of that "kingdom of lost delight," and at the same time reveal eternal truths in the sparest and often the most elegant fashion.

This study explores five different ways in which Willa Cather uses fairy tales in her fiction. Chapter 1, *"The Song of the Lark:* Willa Cather's Cinderella Story," demonstrates Cather's specific use of "Cinderella," as well as the general characteristics of fairy tale in this novel. Thea, like Cinderella, rises from rags to riches. Fred Ottenburg, the "beer prince," first awakens her to the passion which is transformed into the grand passion of her own art.

Chapter 2, *"My Ántonia:* Jim Burden's Fairy-Tale Vision," explores Cather's use of fairy tale to designate a particular romantic perspective a character has of the world. Jim Burden sees the fairy-tale hero journey of his past in the clear colors, simple and definite lines, juxtaposed oppositions, and the motifs and images of fairy tale.

Chapter 3, "The Fairy-Tale Substructure in *My Mortal Enemy,*" shows how "The Sleeping Beauty" and "Snow White" are actually an integral part of the structure of *My Mortal Enemy.* This chapter concentrates on Cather's use of fairy tale in structure and symbol.

Chapter 4, "From Legend to Fairy Tale in *Death Comes for the Archbishop,*" shows how a common fairy-tale pattern lies just below the surface of this novel. The primary story line in *Archbishop* is remarkably close to an age-old motif called "Two Brothers." This motif fits like a kind of transparency on *Archbishop,* adding yet another dimension to this wonderfully dense work. The relationship between fairy tale and legend is also explored in this chapter.

Chapter 5, *"Shadows on the Rock:* Willa Cather's Fairy Tale," shows how Cather gathered all of her knowledge of fairy tale together and used it to create a novel which is itself almost a fairy tale. Cécile Auclair is Cather's fairy-tale princess, and surrounding her are all the trappings of fairy tale, including a prince (Pierre Charron); a magician (Auclair, who is an apothecary); a Gothic rock-set city, surrounded by water like a castle moat and crowned by a palace; and a story which ends "happily ever after."

The work of Max Lüthi and Bruno Bettelheim was most helpful in this project. Bettelheim, in *The Uses of Enchantment,* uses Lüthi's work extensively, adapting Lüthi's interpretations and analyses of fairy tales to his own Freudian perspective. Bettelheim has been criticized for this narrow perspective, perhaps because the Freudians are out of favor at the moment; yet when we see how he imaginatively, and often playfully, manipulates the tales for his own purposes, we can then take his methods and fit them to our needs.

Jack Zipes uses both Lüthi and Bettelheim in developing his Marxist and feminist interpretations of fairy tales, and he adds yet another valuable perspective. Zipes's feminist perspective was essential in this study of Cather's use of the tales, since Cather, like Zipes, so clearly saw the negative dimension in the rigid gender roles embodied in the tales. Zipes's work helped me to explore Cather's thought processes in this direction, even though applying Zipes's Marxist rendition to Cather seems to me farfetched. If a Marxist dimension exists in Willa Cather's work, we can be reasonably sure, since we are familiar with her opinions in this area, that Marxism was not intentional. I owe a debt to each of these scholars. In addition to being intellectually sound, each of them takes a real delight in the tales themselves. Their own work is not only reliable, but a pleasure to read.

The approach I have taken in this study is a narrow one. Willa Cather's work is so much richer, denser, and grander than this study suggests; in order to prove my point I had to confine myself to my own "Birdseye." The outcome, however, is exciting. Scholars have not yet begun to fathom the extent to which fairy tales shape the human imagination, how they underlie our literature as well as our lives.

1

The Song of the Lark:
Willa Cather's Cinderella Story

Nowhere in Willa Cather's major works are there more specific references to fairy tale than in her third novel, *The Song of the Lark*. Knowing Cather's habit of dropping clues that are important keys to the understanding of the work, we cannot then ignore more than a dozen references to fairy tale in *Lark*. When he reviewed the novel in *Smart Set* in 1915, H. L. Mencken called it "one more version, with a few changes, of the ancient fable of Cinderella, probably the oldest of the world's love stories and surely the most steadily popular" (Schroeter 7). When *Lark* is addressed with "Cinderella" in mind, we can see that this tale, as well as the more general characteristics of fairy tale, play an essential part in the structure and the interpretation of the novel. *Lark* accurately triggered "Cinderella" in Mencken's mind in more far-reaching ways than he may have understood himself.

Anyone as well acquainted with the tales as we know Cather was would have known "Cinderella" thoroughly, perhaps in several versions. Certainly she would have known both Perrault's and the Grimms'. Bruno Bettelheim reminds us that "Cinderella" is a story about "wishes coming true, of the humble being elevated, of true merit being recognized even when hidden under rags, of virtue rewarded and evil punished" (*B* 239). Unlike "The Sleeping Beauty" and "Snow White"—two equally famous fairy tales upon which Cather draws extensively in *My Mortal Enemy,* and in which the princess is traditionally passive—"Cinderella" is a tale in which the princess *acts:* "essentially it is through her own efforts, and because of the person she is, that Cinderella is able to transcend magnificently her degraded state, despite what appear as insurmountable obstacles" (*B* 243). In addition, "Cinderella" is also the classic fairy tale of a "princess" whose father loves her best because she is special, and who suffers hardships because she is favored and unique—usually more beautiful, clever, and/or talented than her siblings—and who finally finds her identity when she finds her prince. The oedipal problem lies at the core of "Cinderella," as it does with so many fairy tales. Maria Tatar uses Freud's term "family romance" to denote this situation. Only by solving the oedipal dilemma can life be lived "happily ever after."

Several Cinderella patterns are established in the first pages of the story. Thea's uniqueness is signalled immediately. Dr. Archie has come to deliver Mrs. Kronborg's seventh child, a son, only to find the first, a daughter, neglected and dangerously ill with pneumonia. Dr. Archie says, "But a nice little girl like that—she's worth the whole litter. Where she ever got it from—" (8).[1] He treats eleven-year-old Thea like a little princess, exclaiming to himself, with perversely erotic candor, "What a beautiful thing a little girl's body was,—like a flower . . . so neatly and delicately fashioned, so soft, and so milky white" (10). Like a fairy-tale princess, Thea has golden hair, silky sensitive skin which suffers more than the other children's from the required prickly winter underwear, and a "delicate, tender chin—the one soft touch in her hard little Scandinavian face, as if some fairy godmother had caressed her there and left a cryptic promise" (10). Throughout the novel, this kind of princess imagery is used to describe Thea: her face is "so fair in color," so "full of light . . . she was a flower full of sun" (96); "how white her arms and shoulders were, as if they had been dipped in new milk" (224); her eyes were "like clear green springs in the wood" (224).

Like a proper princess, Thea has "a passion for jewelry. She wanted every shining stone she saw" (4). As a poor music student in Chicago, "she used to brave the biting lake winds and stand gazing at the displays of diamonds and pearls and emeralds; the tiaras and necklaces and earrings, on white velvet" (194). And from the clumsy homemade clothing of Moonstone, Thea eventually dresses in royal gowns: "pale rose-color, with silver butterflies" (278), "the shimmer of [a] pale green dress" (370) which makes her look radiant like "the colors of an apple branch in early spring" (371), or in a clinging green velvet gown from which her throat rises "strong and dazzlingly white" (428).

The seeds are strewn immediately for the oedipal dilemma which underlies the action in *Lark*. Dr. Archie, "[b]ig and handsome and superior to his fellow townsmen" (13), represents Thea's father/king,[2] and the subtle suggestions of erotic desire between them continue into her adulthood. When Thea is thirteen years old, they run into one another one magical July night when the moon is full. Archie sees her "white figure" in the "white moonlight" (80), and together they watch a rabbit which "seemed to be lapping up the moonlight like cream" (80). They sit together in the moonlight, and Thea says to him, "You've got to stay young for me. I'm getting young now, too" (81). Thea explains, "People aren't young when they're children. Look at Thor, now; he's just a little old man. But Gus has a sweetheart, and he's young!" (82). When she is an adult she says to her lover Fred Ottenburg, who is about to meet Archie, "He is almost like my father" (353). Later, secure in her career as a famous opera singer, Thea says in a conversation with Archie, "I think I was in love with you when I was little, but not with any one since then" (456). Archie in turn says to her, "I guess I'm a romantic old fellow, underneath. And you've always been my romance. Those years when you were growing up were my happiest. When I dream about you, I always see you as a little girl" (458). This kind of erotic dialogue runs throughout, until Thea finally commits herself to Fred, "the beer *prince* [my italics]" (266).

Besides Dr. Archie, who is the primary father/king figure, Thea has a series of additional "fathers," who also serve as helpers on her fairy-tale hero journey.[3] Ray Kennedy, the romantic thirty-year-old railroad man, plans to marry twelve-year-old Thea when she is old enough, and "keep her like a queen" (53). Ray is a "loyal-hearted fellow. . . . one of the step-children of Fortune," who had "brought with him from all his wanderings . . . a high standard of personal honor, [and] a sentimental veneration for all women" (51). Ray is typical of the adventurer who wins the hand of the princess, and thus he plays prince as well as father/king, indicating again an Oedipal complication. Chivalrous, knight-like Ray says that Thea "wasn't meant for common men" (147); rather, "[s]he was like a wedding cake, a thing to dream on" (147). He envisions her "with diamonds on her neck and a tiara in her yellow hair, with all the people looking at her" (148). Ray Kennedy dies in a railroad accident when Thea is fifteen years old, the age when most fairy-tale heroines cross the threshold into adulthood. He leaves his insurance money to her with instructions that she use it to further her musical training. This money enables her to leave Moonstone and to begin the journey which ends in self-discovery—when "desire becomes creation" and her passion is turned into art. Ray Kennedy's prophetic last words to Thea are, "She's a queen!" (149).

Wuench, "the wandering music teacher" (23) who first awakens Thea to music and to her own talent, is another of Thea's "fathers." In a sense, he is the magician who activates the gift of the special child. Thea knows that Wuench is "the only one who can teach me what I want to know" (82). Wuench himself is a kind of caricature, like those found in fairy tale. "Wuench was short and stocky, with something rough and bear-like about his shoulders. His face was a dark, bricky red, deeply creased rather than wrinkled, and his skin was like loose leather over his neck band. . . . His hair was cropped close; iron-gray bristles on a bullet-like head" (26). He wears slippers and a thread-bare jacket. Wuench, too, feels an unnatural attraction towards Thea. He thinks to himself:

What was it she reminded him of? . . . a thin glass full of sweet-smelling, sparkling Moselle wine. He seemed to see such a glass before him, in the arbor, to watch the bubbles rising and breaking, like the silent discharge of energy in the nerves and brain, the rapid florescence in young blood—Wuench felt ashamed and dragged his slippers along the path to the kitchen, his eyes on the ground. (30)

Wuench tells Thea that some people "have nothing inside them. . . . They are like the ones in the 'Märchen,' a grinning face and hollow in the insides. These people do not know the secrets" (78). Thea and Wuench both know that she, unlike the *Märchen,* or fairy tales—simplified and silhouetted stories— harbors an artist's intensity and passion. Instead of remaining the equivalent of a fairy-tale princess, the object of everyone's romantic dream, Thea eventually assumes a larger stature and becomes goddess-like, worthy of her name's suggestion. This inner growth is manifested externally, when Thea begins to outgrow her clothes, and even her childhood bed.[4] It is Wuench who gives Thea the key to her art, not only in appreciating her talent and teaching her what he himself knows, but instilling in her the idea that desire is creation, the governing axiom of her life.

Most interesting in the light of fairy tale is the incident in which Wuench, in a fit of drunken madness, chops down the dovecote in the Kohler's garden. In one version of the tale, Cinderella hides from the prince in a dovecote when she flees from the ball. Her father chops down the dovecote. In yet another version, the prince performs this act, but both find that she has fled. The doves themselves are associated with magic—they come to Cinderella's aid, for example, in helping her to divide the lentils from the ashes, one of the impossible tasks which her stepmother throws at her. They also provide her with the ball clothes, including the symbol-laden slippers; they warn the prince that her stepsisters are impostors by pointing out the blood dripping from their feet mutilated to fit the glass slipper; and they peck out the stepsisters' eyes in punishment. In Bettelheim's opinion,

> Cinderella must relinquish her belief in and reliance on the help of magic objects if she is to live well in the world of reality. The father seems to understand this, and so he cuts down her hiding places: no more hiding among the ashes, but also no more seeking refuge from reality in magic places. From now on Cinderella will exist neither far below her true status nor way above it. (*B* 264)

In Thea's situation, the implication seems to be that Wuench, her father/king, knows Thea must begin to take charge of her own life; even though her task might be superhuman, she must undertake it herself, through her own energy, will, and talent.

Doves and swallows, which are often interchangeable in fairy tale, are found throughout *Lark.* Thea is finally associated not with these timid, nesting birds, but rather with the golden eagle in Panther Canyon, which soars alone above them all, symbolizing "[e]ndeavor, achievement, desire, glorious striving of human art!" (321).

Harsanyi, Thea's music teacher in Chicago, is yet another father figure. Just as she inadvertantly has captured Dr. Archie, Ray Kennedy, and Wuench,

Thea also captures Harsanyi:

> He had learned that one must take where and when one can the mysterious mental irritant that rouses one's imagination; that it is not to be had by order. . . . Under her crudeness and brusque hardness, he felt there was a nature quite different, of which he never got so much as a hint except when she was at the piano, or when she sang. It was toward this hidden creature that he was trying, for his own pleasure, to find his way. In short, Harsanyi looked forward to his hour with Thea for the same reason that poor Wuench had sometimes dreaded his; because she stirred him more than anything she did could adequately explain. (190)

Throughout the novel there are erotic undertones in the males' response to Thea; that desire/creation which they intuit in her—her "second self" (217)—and respond to is mingled with sexual desire. Harsanyi refines Thea's musical talent, directing her towards the cultivation of her natural gift—her voice—rather than the piano. At one point Harsanyi says to Thea, "Shipwrecks come and go, *Märchen* come and go, but the river keeps right on. There you have your open, flowing tone" (190). Fairy tales, or *Märchen,* are stories which end—the princess and prince live happily ever after—but the river, an ancient symbol of rebirth, rejuvenation, and continuity, which comes to be associated with Thea's voice and with art, flows on forever.

Cather describes Harsanyi with care, and makes his single eye a significant detail. Cather clearly had Wotan in mind here, the one-eyed father of the gods in Wagner's *Ring* saga.[5] Wotan is the biological father of Sieglinde in Wagner's *Die Walküre,* the operatic role that makes Thea famous. Fred Ottenburg, Thea's symbolic "prince," is also a music pupil of Harsanyi/Wotan. In many ways Fred is Thea's counterpart, the Siegmund to her Sieglinde, twins/lovers "fathered" by Harsanyi/Wotan. Fred, like Thea, is a Nordic blonde, a godlike "gleaming, florid young fellow. His hair [was] thick and yellow . . . and he wore a closely trimmed beard, long enough to curl on the chin a little" (267). His eyebrows are thick and yellow, his eyes are a lively blue, and, like Thea, he is full of natural energy and exuberance. Fred is often Thea's accompanist on the piano, a fact which further suggests that they are conceptually linked.

The most common age in fairy tale for the incident to occur which plunges a child into adulthood is fifteen.[6] Cather tells us first of all: "By the time Thea's fifteenth birthday came round, she was established as a music teacher in Moonstone" (105); she is no longer a schoolgirl, but has an adult vocation. And it is "soon after Thea's fifteenth birthday" (135) that the filthy tramp with his clown suit and box of rattlesnakes drowns himself in the town water tank, polluting the water supply and causing the death of several citizens. Haunted by the figure of the tramp, the despair and defeat he represents, Thea cries, and Dr. Archie notes that he has never seen her cry before.[7] Thea is fifteen, too, when Ray Kennedy dies. Like many a fairy-tale heroine, Thea is fifteen when she loses her innocence, in this case symbolized by incidents which instruct her about defeat and death. Thea must wait a few years for death's conquerors—love and sex.

Like many a fairy-tale princess, Thea is associated with the moon, a major symbol of death and rebirth. She remains forever a child of Moonstone; she sleeps when she is in Moonstone in a tiny, cave-like room, "right in the moonlight. My window comes down to the floor, and I can look at the sky all night" (84). On many summer nights, Thea runs around the town in the moonlight, "with a desire to run and run about those quiet streets until she wore out her shoes" (140).[8] Afterwards, "she lay on the floor in the moonlight, pulsing with ardor and anticipation" (140).

Like the moon, Thea is reborn again and again. One of the most portentous of these rebirths takes place at the Mexican ball, just after Thea's return from Chicago. Interestingly, Thea has been reading *Anna Karenina,* fascinated by the first scene in which "[i]t was the night of the ball in Moscow" (132).[9] In her own Mexican ball, where "the rhythm of the music was smooth and engaging, the men were graceful and courteous" (230), the scene gradually assumes the mood and meaning of ritual. Thea wears a white organdy dress, and her white skin and yellow hair set her apart from the dark Mexicans. Two young men, dressed like twins, dance with her and attend to her. "They were handsome, smiling youths, of eighteen and twenty, with pale-gold skins, smooth cheeks, aquiline features, and wavy black hair, . . . dressed alike, in black velvet jackets and soft silk shirts, with opal shirt-buttons and flowing black ties looped through gold rings" (230).[10] Like courtiers, they are dazzled by the princess's beauty: "her hair and fair skin bewitched them" (230). When they aren't dancing with Thea, their eyes follow her over the dark heads of their partners. "'Blanco y oro, semejante la Pascua!' (White and gold, like Easter!)" (230), they worshipfully exclaim to one another about Thea. For the evening, Thea incarnates the reborn goddess.

The "handsome and adoring" (231) twin princes tell Thea that their surname, *Ramas,* means "branch" in Spanish, and that "[o]nce when they were little lads their mother took them along when she went to help the women decorate the church for Easter. Someone asked her whether she had brought any flowers, and she replied that she had brought her 'ramas'" (231). Close to midnight, the brothers escort Thea outside, where she sits on the velvet coat of Felipe, and wears the identical velvet coat of Silvo, while they lie—the "Ramas"—on either side of her. Significantly, Johnny Tellamantez calls them "'los acolitos,' the altar-boys" (231). Cather has created here an altar: Thea, goddess of rebirth, is the center, with votive "branches" on either side. The ambience of the scene is worshipful, replete with mystery and magic. Voices are low, the moonlight bright, the "moonflowers over Mrs. Tellemantez's door . . . wide open and of an unearthly white. The moon itself looked like a great pale flower in the sky" (232).

Just after midnight, Johnny, carrying his guitar,[11] approaches Thea as if she were sacred. Thea begins to sing, and the dark faces about her become like moonflowers, reflecting the moonlight, while she herself becomes the moon. Silvo "lay looking at the moon, under the impression that he was still looking at Thea" (232). Thea then sings with Johnny and a Mexican baritone. Her voice soars above the others, "like a fountain jet, shot up into the light. . . . How it leaped from among those dusky male voices! How it played in and about and over them, like a goldfish darting among the creek minnows, like a yellow butterfly soaring above a swarm of dark ones" (234). The Kohlers, listening in the bedroom of their house nearby, say, "Die Thea. . . . Ach, wunderschon!" (234)—the Goddess, wonderful! Unlike Cinderella at the prince's ball, or Anna Karenina who meets Vronsky at the ball in Moscow, Thea's night at the ball awakens her not to the love of a man, but to the self-fulfillment of her own art.

Thea is again reborn in Panther Canyon, a section burgeoning with the elements of fairy tale and myth. Exhausted by a hard winter studying voice in Chicago, depleted by a throat infection, "dead tired" (288), as Fred remarks to her, Thea spends a summer restoring herself at Fred's family ranch in Arizona. To get to Panther Canyon, Thea must travel through the Navajo pine forests, analogous to the fairy-tale forests where protagonists go to rediscover themselves. Signaling its importance, Cather tells us that this "was the first great forest she [Thea] had ever seen"; that she "seemed to fall from sleep directly into the forest" (295); and that the forest closes behind the wagon which carries Thea to the canyon, indicating irrevocable passage to a new phase. Thea's "student life closed behind her, like the forest" (296). She "seemed to be taking very little through the wood with her. The personality of which she was so tired seemed to let go of her" (296).[12]

Thea climbs into her bed at the end of the journey, and finds for the first time since she left Moonstone that "[d]arkness had once again the sweet wonder that it had in childhood" (296). She wakes to days in which her life once again, as in childhood, becomes "simple and full of light" (297), suffused with sunshine, where she loses her sense of self in the experience of being. "She could become a mere receptacle for heat, or become a color, like the bright lizards that darted about on the hot stones outside her door; or she could become a continuous repetition of sound, like the cicadas" (300). Thea lies in her "nest in a high cliff, full of sun," and experiences that sense of peace which Jim Burden feels in his grandmother's garden:

> I kept as still as I could. Nothing happened. I did not expect anything to happen. I was something that lay under the sun and felt it, like the pumpkins, and I did not want to be anything more. I was entirely happy. Perhaps we feel like that when we die and become a part of something entire, whether it is sun and air, or goodness and knowledge. At any rate, that is happiness; to be dissolved into something complete and great. (*MA* 18)

Maria Tatar tells us that the hero of fairy tale "invariably finds shelter and substance in nature" (73), a statement which is true of both Jim Burden and Thea, as well as Latour in *Death Comes for the Archbishop,* another Cather novel which contains fairy-tale ingredients. Thea spends hours, day after day, in her warm cave, often becoming fetus-like, responding only to sensation, pondering what it would be like "to dream one's life out in some cleft in the world" (301)—in other words, to resist rebirth.

Thea takes ritual baths in the river in the bottom of the canyon, climbing up afterwards to her sunlit womb-like cave in the Cliff Dwellers' ruins. At the end of the summer Fred Ottenburg arrives, and Thea's period of "Sleeping Beauty"[13] stillness ends. Fred, "the beer prince," Thea's "instrument" (315), completes her awakening to sensual passion which was begun by nature,[14] opening her, finally, to that grander passion which is art.

In using "Cinderella" as a key to *Lark,* we must address the tale's primary and pivotal symbol—Cinderella's slipper. Throughout folktale history, a slipper, which is a major fairy-tale motif, has had a sexual connotation, consistently representing the vagina.[15] Bettelheim informs us that in all versions of "Cinderella," an ancient tale which probably originated in China, the fairy-tale prince cherishes the real princess's slipper, which is always made of a some precious material. "This tells her in symbolic form that he loves her femininity as represented by the symbol of the vagina" (*B* 270). And furthermore, "all over the world in much loved stories the female slipper has been accepted as a fairy-tale solution to the problem of finding the right Bride" (*B* 269).

The vagina and the slipper are both containers, vessels, protecting sheaths. Cather makes clear the point that Thea's throat is also a vessel, while her voice is likened time and again to a stream or a river. She makes the analogy between Thea's throat and voice and the exquisite pottery made by the Indian women to contain the precious water, the source of "all their customs, ceremonies, and religion" (303). "Their pottery was their most direct appeal to water, the envelope and sheath of the precious element itself" (303). The stream in the bottom of the canyon in which Thea bathes "was the only living thing left of the drama that had been played out in the canyon centuries ago" (304). The bits of shards, remnants of the water-carriers' vessels, are "fragments of their desire" (321). That desire has been channeled into the creation of art. Thea arrives at this understanding one morning while bathing:

> The stream and the broken pottery: what was any art but an effort to make a sheath, a mould in which to imprison for a moment the shining, elusive element which is life itself,—life hurrying past us and running away, too strong to stop, too sweet to lose? The Indian women held it in their jars. . . . In singing, one made a vessel of one's throat and nostrils and held it on one's breath, caught the stream in a scale of natural intervals. (304)

Figure 1.   Cinderella's Flight
An analogy can be drawn between Thea's throat and voice, the
exquisite pottery made by the Indian women to contain the
precious water, and Cinderella's slipper.
(Illustration by G. P. Jacomb Hood, from The Blue Fairy
Book, *ed. Andrew Lang, published by Longmans, Green and
Co., London, 1889; Dover edition, 1965)*

Sharon O'Brien argues persuasively: "Like the Indian women's vessels and the womb with which they are metaphorically associated, Thea's throat can pour forth as well as contain. Her ability to release the voice to the world demonstrates Cather's transformation of a symbol traditionally used to signal female passivity and immanence: Thea's vessel is not a receptacle for male power, but a container for female power" (O'Brien 173). O'Brien concludes that "the woman singer's voice/vessel/womb is Cather's final rival to the male writer's pen/sword/penis" (O'Brien 173).

O'Brien fails here to take into consideration the necessary role of the male. Thea's voice/vessel/womb/slipper both contains and communicates her passion. She cannot take hold and unleash her power, however, without the aid of the symbolic prince, Fred, who "had keys to all the nice places in his pocket" (286). She cannot deliver art any more than a woman can give birth to a child, without male insemination. Thea must first be awakened to sexual passion before she can understand the complexities of that grand passion which is art. If "voice is personality" (355), her own a "vitality; a lightness in the body and a driving power in the blood" (307), then Thea discovers that personality in her passionate involvement with Fred. Fred says to her, "It's only since you've known me that you've let yourself be beautiful" (356). He adds gratuitously, "Since [you've known me] you've come into your personality" (355).

At this point, Thea the princess completely transcends her fairy-tale role and assumes the proportions of a Norse goddess. She exudes "muscular energy and audacity,—a kind of brilliancy of motion,—of a personality that carried across big spaces and expanded among big things" (320). In one scene she is unmistakably a Wagnerian Rhinemaiden: Fred "saw Thea standing on the edge of a projecting crag"; she "threw her arm over her head," and Fred thinks, "She'll begin to pitch rocks on me if I don't move." He addresses the figure on the crag: "You are the sort that used to run wild in Germany, dressed in their hair and a piece of skin" (320). Thea and Fred become Sieglinde and Siegmund in Panther Canyon, "two figures nimbly moving in the light, both slender and agile, entirely absorbed in their game. They looked like two boys. Both were hatless and both wore shirts. . . . Fred was teaching her to throw a heavy stone like a discus" (310). They climb, fence, and ride together, providing for one another "a rhythm of feeling and action" (316). Fred becomes Thea's complement as well as her "instrument" (315), the brother/lover who is the necessary other half of her self.[16]

The message in this novel is clear: without her male half, the "prince" who completes her in all ways, including fulfilling her sexually, Thea would remain incomplete, and would never fully assume her own power. Sex is as important here as it is in any fairy tale, connecting the princess to love, to death, to the human condition.

The course of true art, like true love, however, never runs smooth. Thea discovers that her prince, her lover, her "other" is married to someone else. Fred's is a bad marriage to a cruel, psychotic woman, one into which he was trapped as a young man and from which he cannot untangle himself. He in every way loves Thea, but cannot marry her, nevertheless. Thea borrows money from Dr. Archie, who again comes to her rescue, and sails for Germany, where she eventually becomes a great Wagnerian singer. We are told in the epilogue to the novel, which takes place in Moonstone many years later, that Thea and Fred, at some indeterminate time, marry. The ceremony, recalled by Thea's ever-admiring Aunt Tillie, befitted the wedding of a princess to a prince: Thea "came down the stairs in the wedding robe embroidered in silver, with a train so long it took six women to carry it" (487). The assumption is that they lived happily ever after, since we know no more. But returned to the simpler formula, Thea Kronborg's story becomes Aunt Tillie's fairy tale. Tillie had "always insisted, against all evidence, that life was full of fairy tales" (489).

In addition to the general Cinderella plot line, *Lark* contains fairy-tale motifs and characters. Thea's Aunt Tillie is a witch-like character, one of those people who, "foolish about the more obvious things of life are apt to have peculiar insight into what lies beyond the obvious. The old woman who can never learn not to put the kerosene can on the stove, may yet be able to tell fortunes, to persuade a backward child to grow, to cure warts, or to tell people what to do with a young girl who has gone melancholy" (66). Tillie wants Thea to have a ball gown to take with her when she leaves for Chicago. Thea gets, instead, "a dress with a piece of every known fabric in it somewhere" (173), a dress of patches, like Cinderella's.

Mrs. Archie is also a stock fairy-tale character, a kind of woman ogre, in the same class as the Grimms' stepmothers, mothers-in-law, and witches. Belle White, with a "train of suitors" (34), begins to "shrink in face and stature" as soon as she is married until nothing is left of her spirit but a "little screech" (35). She burns to death in witch fashion, while polishing furniture with kerosene, igniting herself and her whole house. The townspeople say, "Nothing but a powerful explosive *could* have killed Mrs. Archie" (389). Female ogres like Mrs. Archie are usually associated with food, often with its denial, as in "Hansel and Gretel," where both the mother and the witch are food perverts (Tatar 140). Mrs. Archie withholds food, giving Dr. Archie "miserable scraps" (33) when he comes home for lunch, and Thea the smallest basket to fill from their abundant strawberry patch.

One of the most significant fairy-tale motifs in *Lark,* and a key to the novel's meaning, is Thea's dream: "In one dream she was looking into a hand-glass and thinking that she was getting better-looking, when the glass began to grow smaller and smaller and her own reflection to shrink, until she realized that she was looking into Ray Kennedy's eyes, seeing her face in that look of his" (381). The eyes in which Thea sees herself then become Fred Ottenburg's.

The echoes of "Snow White" are unmistakable here.[17] Gilbert and Gubar argue that the voice in the mirror is a male voice: "His surely is the voice of the looking glass, the patriarchal voice of judgement that rules the Queen's—and every woman's—self-evaluation" (*Madwoman* 39).

Thea is a male-oriented female, like Myra Henshawe and Marian Forrester, two "princesses" who also use men to achieve their own ends. The women in her life are either admirers like Aunt Tillie and Mrs. Andersen, or enemies like her sister Anna and Lily Fisher. If "[it] takes a great many people to make one Brünnehilde" (465), most of these people are males, her "whistling posts" (378). As we are told, Thea "would never have loved a man from whom she could not learn a great deal" (378).

Viewing *The Song of the Lark* through fairy tale adds a new dimension to the novel. Thea, like Cinderella, rises from rags to riches through her connection with a "prince." Perhaps a subtle twist on the traditional fairy tale is the princess's manipulation of the prince for her own grander ends. Unlike Myra Henshawe, who makes romantic love her life's passion, Thea Kronborg uses it as a stepping stone to transcendence. And like Cécile Auclair, Thea Kronborg provides civilization with that continuity which is art.

My Ántonia: **Jim Burden's Fairy-Tale Vision**

Willa Cather's use of fairy tale is less apparent in *My Ántonia* than in its predecessor, *The Song of the Lark.* In the later *My Mortal Enemy* and *Shadows on the Rock,* the tales are again an integral part of the text, but in *Ántonia* their use is more subtle and less conscious. Still, the text of *Ántonia* not only contains a number of specific fairy-tale allusions, but also provides many ingredients of fairy tales themselves. My contention is that Cather was often aware of her use of fairy tales, used them for specific reasons, and that this usage developed into a steadily elaborating technique. We must, then, determine where such allusions and ingredients are located in the text of *My Ántonia,* how they are used at this stage in her career, and why she used them.

When we apply Stith Thompson's method of classifying folk tales, the genre to which fairy tale belongs, to *Ántonia,* we can begin to see the extent to which Cather uses the ingredients of fairy tale in this novel. Thompson breaks all folk tales into a "type" (constituted by the major story line which conforms to a classified pattern) and into "motifs" (those individual strands and elements which make up the story).[1]

The narrative "type," following Thompson's system of classification, in *My Ántonia* is the hero journey, fairy tale's most common plot for a tale in which the protagonist is male rather than female.[2] "The fairy-tale hero . . . leaves home to wander out into the world, in a sense out into the void" (*LF* 136). In the novel's main narrative line, Jim Burden, recently orphaned, embarks on a journey from West Virginia to begin a new life with his grandparents in Nebraska.[3] Like most fairy-tale heroes, Jim is an orphan; and as such has been estranged from his family by forces beyond his control. Thus of necessity he has set out in search of a new identity. Jim's journey is in every way a mythic journey into the void, literally one without guideposts, for he feels "the world was left behind, that we had got over the edge of it, and were outside man's jurisdiction" (7).

On this journey, true to Joseph Campbell's hero journey formula—which is identical to the journey of a fairy-tale hero—Jim crosses water, "so many rivers that he was dull to them" (5). Accompanying him are a classic set of *three* guides and protectors: Jake Marpole, one of his father's farm hands who goes West to work for Jim's grandfather; a friendly and helpful passenger conductor on the Western bound train, "who knew all about the country to which we were going and gave us a great deal of advice" (4), and who wears rings, badges, and cuff-buttons engraved with hieroglyphics which give him the air of mystery appropriate to a guide on a hero journey; and Otto Fuchs, Grandfather Burden's hired man, whose scarred cheek and moustache twisted like little horns give him "the face of a desperado" (6). When Jim reaches his destination he feels "erased, blotted out" (8) by the vastness of the Nebraska prairies. The prairies here are synonymous with the forest of fairy tale; being lost in a forest is the ancient symbol in mythology for the need to find oneself. In fact, Cather uses this motif in exactly the same way in *Archbishop,* where the narrative opens with Latour being lost in a "desert of ovens" (20).[4] Like many a fairy-tale hero, Jim must find his way out of the wilderness and begin forging a new identity for himself by creating his own boundaries.

Jim wakes in a little room "scarcely larger than the bed that held me" (8), with his kindly grandmother looking down at him. The enclosed space of this little room is juxtaposed against the limitlessness of the prairie—total safety and closely defined boundaries against formless danger and the endless space which threatens annihilation. This same juxtaposition is a common occurrence in fairy tale; although not classified by Thompson in his index, it is clearly a significant fairy-tale motif. Goldilocks, for example, is lost in the forest before she stumbles upon the house of the three bears. The same juxtaposition is found in "The Robber Bridegroom," "Hansel and Gretel," and "Red Riding Hood," to mention a few famous tales, although in these tales the enclosed spaces are sinister rather than safe. Cather herself uses this motif again in *Archbishop,* when Latour and Vaillent are lost on the road to Mora and come upon the house of subhuman Buck Scales, an "ugly, evil-looking man with a snake-like neck, terminating in a small, long head" (67). Even a sinister house, however, poses less threat to the hero than being lost in the ego-annihilating forest. The evil contained within the house becomes an obstacle which can be attacked and conquered, as well as a means of providing the tale with a plot. The fairy-tale motif present here in *Ántonia* is this juxtaposition of the unbounded void, represented by the prairies, and the tightly enclosed space, represented by Jim's grandmother's house.

In *The Song of the Lark,* Willa Cather says, "A child's attitude towards everything is an artist's attitude" (460). In her earlier story, "The Treasure of Far Island," she says,

> A child's normal attitude toward the world is that of the artist pure and simple. The rest of us have to do with the solids of this world, whereas only their form and color exist for the painter.

So, in every wood and street and building there are things, not seen by older people at all, which make up their whole desirableness or objectionableness to children. (*SF* 275)

⌊To continue, Cather says that to children the entire external world is valued solely for what it suggests to the imagination, for what it contributes to the intensity of the inner life.⌉

⌈Carrying this definition of a child's vision further, Bruno Bettelheim explains that a child divides the world into polar oppositions, and then sees these oppositions as absolutes in an attempt to create order in the chaos he perceives around him. Cather alludes to this kind of polarization of opposites when she refers to the "desirableness or objectionableness" of things. This child's/artist's ordering of reality, of seeing a world of juxtaposed opposites in simple definite lines and shapes, a world of clear colors without complexity or shadow, is precisely the way in which fairy tale structures the world⌉ Fairy tale, too, "delights . . . in the simple, clearly drawn line" (*LF* 41). And Jim Burden, Cather's narrator in *Ántonia,* who journeys back through memory to his childhood to discover what he had lost as an adult, sees not only as child/artist, but also through the lens of fairy tale.

Jim's childhood world is as "simple . . . but definite" (*Shadows* 64) as the world Cather creates in *Shadows on the Rock,* which I contend is her own attempt to write a fairy tale. In Jim's version, as in fairy tale, "figures are clearly drawn, and details, unless very important, are eliminated" (*B* 8).⌈Objects and people are sharply outlined, but they exist only in outline, colored by clear, primary colors.⌉ The walls of Jim's grandmother's house are white-washed, red geraniums in deep sills stand against white-curtained windows, and bright nickel trims the stove. Grandmother is tall, spare, aproned; she wears a sunbonnet and carries a stout hickory stick for killing rattlesnakes—an absolutely positive and protecting maternal figure. Grandfather has a "beautiful crinkly, snow-white beard," like the beard of an Arabian sheik. His eyes are "bright blue, and had a fresh, frosty sparkle" (12). He wears silver-rimmed spectacles, and his teeth are white and regular. These are figures seen only in outline, the simple and definite vision of a child's eye.

Jim's grandmother and grandfather are common fairy-tale figures. In one of the most familiar tales in which these two figures are found, "The Gingerbread Man," an old woman and an old man, wanting a little boy, create him from gingerbread.[6] The smell of gingerbread even permeates Jim's grandmother's kitchen on the morning of his arrival. One cannot help but suspect that this particular tale was hovering in Jim Burden's/Willa Cather's mind when this scene was written. This scene itself verges on the quaint and overly-sentimental. Only when we understand it as Jim Burden's attempt to see this most significant scene in his childhood through the eyes of the romantic little boy that he was, does the scene become more complex, and we appreciate the artistry involved in its conception.

As the first-person narrator, Jim Burden often uses specific fairy-tale analogies. On his first trip across the red grass, he says of the cottonwoods that "the yellow leaves and shining white bark made them look like the gold and silver trees in fairy tales" (21). We should note here that two characters named Jim Burden are present in this novel; Jim Burden as an adult journeys through memory into his past, where he creates Jim Burden, the ten-year-old child, and brings him through memory to the conclusion of the novel, where the two Jim Burdens become one. Thus *My Ántonia,* like most fairy tales, is essentially the story of the integration of a personality.

In taking this journey through memory, Jim is attempting to link himself once again with an idyllic past, where "[e]verything was as it should be" (346), and to anchor this past in permanence. Gold and silver trees in fairy tales are symbols of permanence, attempting to make ever-changing nature unchanging. We find these images suggesting Jim Burden's longing for permanence throughout the novel. He says, "The barks of the oaks turned red as *copper.* There was a shimmer of *gold* on the brown river. Out in the stream the sandbars glittered like *glass* [my emphasis]" (244). When Ántonia takes up with the other hired girls, Jim says that he "used to think with pride that Ántonia, like Snow-White in the fairy tale, was still fairest of them all" (215).[7] Snow White is yet another image of permanence, frozen as she is in perfection until the prince's kiss arouses her to love, to sex, and to death. Cather uses this imagery of permanence once again in *Shadows,* where she again attempts to anchor herself in a permanent childhood world.[8]

Perhaps the most interesting of these images of permanence is Cather's famous plough against the sun. Jim, Ántonia, and three of the hired girls are picnicking near a river, a place symbolizing childhood that Cather has written about before in "The Treasure of Far Island" and "The Enchanted Bluff."[9] Jim is now fifteen,[10] and Lena Lingard, one of the hired girls, says to him, "The trouble with you, Jim, is that you're romantic" (229), reminding us yet once again of Jim's romantic outlook. Jim still insists upon seeing with a child's vision, trying to deny that his world has become more complex.

In *The Professor's House,* Godfrey St. Peter says that "adolescence grafted a new creature onto the original one, and that the complexion of a man's life was largely determined by how well or ill his original self and his nature as modified by sex rubbed on together" (267). Jim Burden, at this point in the earlier novel, is in the process of having his nature modified by sex. We can assume that the graft fails to bond, however, since Jim's eventual marriage is in every way sterile, and he returns to his childhood in search of his "original self," his most real self.

The adolescent Jim dreams of Lena coming to kiss him "across the stubble barefoot, in a short skirt, with a curved reaping-hook in her hand, and she was flushed like the dawn, with a kind of luminous rosiness all about her" (226). Of Ántonia he dreams a kind of "Jack and Jill" dream, with the sexuality just a little less obvious than in his dream of Lena: "Tony and I were out in the country, sliding down straw-stacks as we used to; climbing up the yellow mountains over and over, and slipping down the smooth sides into soft piles of chaff" (224). Lena's reaping hook suggests the death of childhood innocence, whereas Ántonia's haystacks suggest an evasion of more mature impulses.

When the day of the picnic is over, Jim and the girls see a black iron plough against the molten red of the sun, an image of permanence which, as Jim watches it, slides from view as the sun's "ball dropped and dropped until the red tip went beneath the earth" and "that forgotten plough had sunk back to its own littleness somewhere on the prairie" (245). Similarly, Cather's plough disappearing with the sun also signals the end of Jim's childhood, the end of a vision of the world in which things are simple and definite, as well as the magnitude of the feared and admired phallic plough which will dominate Jim's future. The undercurrents during this picnic are subtly but intensely erotic. In the next chapter Jim comes close to being accidentally raped by Wick Cutter when he takes Ántonia's place in her bed in Cutter's house. For awhile thereafter he blames Ántonia for the loss of his child's vision of the world, saying, "She had let me in for all this disgustingness" (250).

Cather excuses and justifies Jim's fairy-tale vision by telling us first in the introduction that Jim is a romantic, and then alluding to his romantic nature several times during the narration. At this point in the novel, Jim's vision becomes less that of child/artist, and less romantic. Forms and colors are less clear and definite; Jim begins to see "the solids of this world" (*SF* 275), shadows and complexities. Characters no longer seem so grandly scaled. In the last chapter, when Jim rediscovers Ántonia after twenty years, he finds again with her his childhood vision. The last images of the novel, like the first, seem to be out of a child's picture book. "Everything was as it should be: the strong smell of sunflowers and iron weed in the dew, the clear blue and gold of the sky, the evening star, the purr of the milk in the pails, the grunts and squeals of the pigs fighting over their supper" (347).

In the Introduction Cather identifies herself with Jim in a most interesting way. Jim Burden and a character called "I," old friends who grew up in the same prairie town, are traveling West together in "a season of intense heat." They sit in the "observation car" going back through fields of wheat and through their own communal memories. Readers and critics have appropriately assumed that this "I" represents Cather herself; she is thus returning to her own childhood through a fictional character called "Jim Burden," distancing herself through Jim the adult, further yet through Jim the child, and still further through an obscure character called "I." And here again, with Cather and Jim, we have a fairy-tale motif—that of the brother and sister.

Sharon O'Brien argues that Cather was fascinated with the sister/brother bond throughout her life, stemming from her own close relationship with her brothers. O'Brien quotes from Cather: "[T]he strongest and most satisfactory relation of human life [is] the love that sometimes exists between a brother and sister. . . . It is more than a tie of blood; much more" (108). O'Brien asserts that "Cather . . . saw the opposite-sex sibling as embodying a part of the self" (108), representing self, twin, brother, and other. In one of her favorite operas, Wagner's *Die Walküre*, to which she alludes several times in her fiction, a brother and sister pair, Siegmund and Sieglinde, are lovers as well as two parts of the same self.[11] Here again is a universal folklore motif; we recall quickly Hansel and Gretel, the most famous example of this motif in fairy tale. By aligning her female self with Jim Burden in the Introduction, Cather suggests that in order to explore her own childhood, both female and male, herself and her male half, are needed to constitute a whole character, and thus to conjure a more accurate memory. This sister/brother bond is frequently implied between Ántonia and Jim. In the closing scene of the novel, Jim recalls being "bedded down in the straw [with Ántonia], wondering children, being taken we knew not whither" (371), a scene that not only suggests Hansel and Gretel, but also two siblings in the womb.

Sharon O'Brien argues further that the search for the mother is one of the predominant themes in Cather's fiction. From her earliest stories, according to O'Brien, mothers are divided into polar opposites: either cold and narcissistic or loving and self-sacrificing. O'Brien uses fairy tales as an analogy for Cather's treatment of mothers:

> Like fairy tales, which oppose the benevolent fairy godmother to her malevolent opposite and double, the cruel stepmother or vindictive witch, such stories [Cather's early stories] reflect the child's splitting of the mother into "good" and "bad" selves: unable to comprehend how the same person can be both caring and punishing, loving and rejecting, she dissociates loving feelings from the angry ones by constructing two opposed maternal figures. (49)

O'Brien imaginatively interprets Cather's move from Virginia to Nebraska as a recapitulation of the child's first sense of pain and loss—separation from the mother (64), which brings with it both independence and alienation. Virginia thus first represents the good land/mother, Nebraska the bad. On the assumption that this theory is valid, this juxtaposition would then be reversed at the end of *Ántonia;* Ántonia herself comes to represent not only Nebraska, but also the ultimate, all-caring and protecting mother figure, "the closest, realest face, under all the shadows of women's faces, at the very bottom of my memory"

Figure 2. Hansel and Grettel
Hansel and Grettel, the most
famous brother/sister pair in
fairy tale, are echoed in Jim and
Ántonia.
(Illustration by H. J. Ford, from
The Blue Fairy Book, *ed.*
Andrew Lang, published by
Longmans, Green and Co.,
London, 1889; Dover edition,
1965)

(322). Thus Jim, through Ántonia, achieves a kind of reconciliation with a mother substitute.

In *Ántonia,* Cather continues with a pattern that O'Brien observes in the early stories. Jim Burden is in search of his mother, and the mothers he finds—first his grandmother, then Mrs. Harling, and finally Ántonia—are the absolutely good and all-providing mothers characteristic of fairy tale. Indeed, *Ántonia* is as much a book about mothers as *Shadows,* in which Cather again takes up the theme of mothers as well as fathers.

Bettelheim argues that most fairy tales place the story not in time or place of external reality, but in a state of mind—that of the young in spirit. He says that a fairy tale is "set in a state of mind," the voyage is one "into the interior of a mind" (62). Normal logic and causation are suspended until the conclusion, when the hero returns to a happy reality. Clearly this pattern is Jim's in *My Ántonia.* At the end of the story, Jim is reunited with Ántonia, who represents "the country, the conditions, the whole adventure of our childhood" (Introduction). We don't question the happiness at the conclusion of *Ántonia;* we do, however, continue to question the "reality."

In Bettelheim's opinion, underlying all fairy tale is the struggle with the oedipal dilemma; however valid and useful a system, this is only one way to view fairy tale. But when looking at *Ántonia* from Bettelheim's perspective, Jim's oedipal dilemma is resolved when he becomes at the end one of "Cuzak's boys"; he has the sense of being reunited with the mother in a relationship without oedipal strains. His final image of being "bedded down in the straw" with Ántonia when they were "wondering children" (371) gives him "the sense of coming home to myself and of having found out what a little circle man's experience is" (371). The void has at last been conquered; Jim Burden has found his boundaries—symbolized by this bed of straw in the prairie/forest. If, as Bettelheim tells us, all fairy tales concern the attempt of a hero to integrate a personality (*B* 90), then Jim Burden has succeeded in his search for inner integration. As a fairy-tale hero, he has discovered himself.

Cather's inset tale of the two Russians, Pavel and Peter, who feed the bride and groom to the wolves, is a fairy tale complete within itself, set as it is within Jim Burden's hero journey. The major motif here is that of two brothers who are in every way opposites. Pavel has a "great frame, with big, knotty joints" (33) and a wasted look, while Peter is "short, bow-legged, and as fat as butter" (34). Cather uses a variation of this motif again with her two priests in *Archbishop*. Lüthi labels this kind of narrative a tale of "succession"; "The Gingerbread Man" also follows this same narrative pattern. One after another the sledges are lost to the wolves, until finally Pavel lightens the last sledge by throwing the bride and groom to the wolves.

Paul Schrach informs us that German immigrants brought wolf stories to the Great Plains, and that Cather probably heard this directly from settlers in Nebraska.[12] She herself says in an early interview that the old women among her foreign neighbors, who spoke very little English, "somehow managed to tell me a great many stories about the old country" (*KA* 448). We might assume that the tale of Pavel and Peter is one of these stories. Cather makes this tale a part of America's heritage by imprinting it in the minds of the new generation, Jim and Ántonia. She demonstrates this cultural assimilation of stories by telling us that Jim, before he went to sleep, "often found [himself] in a sledge drawn by three horses, dashing through a country that looked something like Nebraska and something like Virginia" (61). We should note here that in his dream Jim is thus in a sledge divested of its bride and groom. This image illustrates the way in which fairy tale may become part of the mental makeup of an individual, as well as the characterizations of a novel.

Another major motif in *My Ántonia* is hero as "dragonslayer" (50), a term Cather herself uses in the text. Jim and Ántonia are playing in the prairie dog city when they encounter an enormous rattlesnake which seems like "the ancient, eldest Evil," a creature "which has left horrible unconscious memories in all warm-blooded life" (47). Jim seizes a shovel and kills the snake, proving his manhood to Ántonia and to himself. In the Freudian systems of twentieth-century readers, of course, he again kills the great phallus. According to fairy tale, this battle with the dragon "means ultimately the internal struggle with one's drives and feelings. . . . Modern psychology believes that our own unconscious can appear to us as an animal or a dragon. It prepares to devour us, but in our battle with it, we win the princess" (*LO* 80).[13] The sexual undertones are clear here. Jim's dilemma is the age-old Freudian one—that in winning the princess, Ántonia, he is winning his mother, a guilt that he resolves at the conclusion by regressing to a prepubertal self which is innocent of sexual temptation.

Fairy-tale motifs are also in evidence in this novel in the images which Cather uses.[14] Mrs. Shimerda gives the Burdens mushrooms gathered in "some deep Bohemian forest" (79). Mushrooms and toadstools from a forest are magic objects in fairy tale, primary motifs. Jim describes the Christmas tree as "the talking tree of the fairy tale" (83). Mr. Shimerda kneels in front of the tree in prayer; a praying figure under a magic tree is a common one in fairy tale. Ghosts have substance in fairy tale; Jim feels that Mr. Shimerda's ghost takes shelter from the snow in his grandmother's warm kitchen. Large birds symbolize evil in fairy tale; thus: "Misfortune seemed to settle like an evil bird on the roof of the log house and to flop its wings there, warning human beings away" (53).

The wind is personified in fairy tale, and Jim Burden tells us: "The wind shook the doors and windows impatiently, then swept on again, singing through the big spaces. Each gust, as it bore down, rattled the panes, and swelled off like the others. They made me think of defeated armies, retreating; or of ghosts who were trying desperately to get in for shelter, and then went moaning on" (53). At the end of chapter two, all nature is personified: giant grasshoppers perform acrobatic feats, the wind sings a humming tune, and squadrons of red bugs move around Jim. And feathers used as an analogy for snow is a familiar motif: "Snow . . . spilled out of heaven, like thousands of feather-beds being emptied" (92).

The "old beggar woman who went about selling herbs and roots she had dug up in the forest" (39) is as familiar in fairy tale as Jim Burden's rosy-cheeked grandparents. And seeds scattered to create a trail is yet another motif, one with which we are most familiar in "Hansel and Gretel"; the Mormons scattered sunflower seeds as they traveled across the prairie, creating the sunflower trail that Jim follows on his pony. Mrs. Cutter is described as "almost a giantess" (211); one young man in Black Hawk is "like the son of a royal house" (202); and the Danish laundry girls have golden hair and cheeks "bright as the brightest wild roses" (202). Lena Lingard is a Cinderella figure: she wears rags to tend the cattle, and her beauty is noticed when she arrives at church in a new dress.

Once one addresses the extent to which Cather uses the elements of fairy tale in *My Ántonia,* one finds it difficult to believe she was not aware of their use. Its most significant use in this novel, however, is in Jim Burden's ordering of reality through fairy tale, in his romantic—or fairy-tale—vision. Jim looks back at his own life as a kind of fairy-tale hero journey, full of the figures and images of the tales—including absolutely good mothers, and a happy resolution at the end of the journey. He sees his past in the simple and definite forms and lines, the clear colors, the juxtaposed absolutes of a fairy tale.

In *The Voyage Perilous: Willa Cather's Romanticism,* Susan J. Rosowski calls *My Ántonia* a novel "about the capacity of the mind to perceive symbols as self-generating sources of meaning" (preface). She argues "that one of the distinguishing features of Cather's romanticism is that she was not nearly so concerned with *what* we see as with the way in which we do so" (preface). The way in which romantic Jim Burden looks at his childhood is with that child's/ artist's eye, which is also the perspective of fairy tale. Jim Burden's symbols, like Nellie Birdseye's in the next novel to be discussed, are the symbols of fairy tale.

3

The Fairy-Tale Substructure in *My Mortal Enemy*

Willa Cather's cryptic novel, *My Mortal Enemy,* has continued to puzzle, frustrate and fascinate readers since its publication in 1926. No matter how hard one probes, still it refuses to completely render up its secrets. If, as David Stouck says, allusions and veiled references count more in this novel than in any of her others (116), we should then address Cather's significant allusions and references to fairy tale within her text in an attempt at further illumination. The novel acquires new meaning when one interprets it specifically through the lens of two fairy tales, "The Sleeping Beauty" and "Snow White," both alluded to in the text.

Stories about princesses such as we find in these two tales, or references to such stories, appear in Cather's earliest as well as her later writing. In addition to publishing her own fairy tale, "The Princess Baladina," Cather reviewed two serialized stories for the *Home Journal* in 1985: *The Princess Aline,* by Richard Harding Davis, published in *Harper's Monthly;* and *Princess Sonia,* by Julia Magruder, published in *Century.* Cather's review of the Magruder story is especially interesting since it describes a plot startlingly similar to *My Mortal Enemy:*

> The girl, Martha, has a rather plain face and a very romantic heart. . . . She is wonderfully drawn to the princess by her beauty, her rank, her talent and the possibilities of her having had a romantic past and being destined for a romantic future. . . . Martha is not exactly fitted to experience a romantic career herself, so she has a habit of becoming desperately interested in other women, of whom she demands that they shall lead romantic lives and let her get a share of the fun and excitement of it second hand. . . . Miss Magruder ha[s] got at it very nicely, that natural admiration that a shy, awkward girl with a soul packed full of things that ought to go only with beauty and grace has for a woman of affairs and experience who has all the physical charms that ha[ve] been denied to her, and, on the other hand, the yearning that a woman of the world who is surfeited with general admiration and tempestuous love has for a single specific affection which can charm and amuse her by its freshness and inexperience. . . . It is a rather strong and beautiful thing, that bond of sympathy which exists between women who are tired of men and very young women who know nothing of them except by hearsay. . . . It is about the only kind of friendship possible between women, and of course when

reduced to the last analysis it is possible only because of their unconscious attitude toward men. The eternal fact of sex seems to be at the bottom of everything. But after people have ceased to seek for love there is one thing that they seem to go on asking for, and that is sympathy. . . .

Of course this friendly business is to be merely an incidental part of the story, but it is well handled and worth considering. . . . It is a rather unimportant phase of life, but all the more important ones have been so grandly treated by our forefathers that about the only thing left to us in this generation is to handle the lesser ones skilfully. (*WP* 152)

Clearly the germs of *My Mortal Enemy* lie in Cather's perceptions about *Princess Sonia*. The relationship between Cather's plain-faced, awkward, and romantic-hearted Nellie Birdseye and charming and worldly Myra Henshawe is too close to the one described in the earlier review to be entirely coincidental. And interestingly, this situation also parallels the plot of Bellini's opera *Norma,* which Cather weaves into her novel. Norma is not a princess but rather a priestess, who worships a male god through the moon. A thread of the story is Norma's relationship with a younger vestal virgin who replaces her in her lover Pollione's affections.

My Mortal Enemy also shows influences of Sarah Orne Jewett's short story, "Martha's Lady," which, according to Sharon O'Brien, Cather treasured, and reread over and over, finally including it in her 1925 edition of Jewett's stories. "Martha's Lady" is the story of two women involved, like Myra and Nellie, in a kind of mother-daughter relationship. Martha gazes into Helena's mirror, which suggests to O'Brien "the daughter's recognition of identity and difference in relation to her mother, her first mirror" (348). We are reminded here that Myra's first glimpse of Nellie is in a mirror. The names, too, bear similarity; Myra and Martha have a phonetic similarity, while Nellie is one of the nick-names for Helena. In all of these stories—"The Sleeping Beauty," "Snow White," "Princess Sonia," "Martha's Lady," *Norma,* and *My Mortal Enemy*— "the eternal fact of sex seems to be at the bottom of everything." And in each, the relationship between an older, powerful woman and a younger one energizes the story. Thus, all are variations of a similar tale.

This pattern of recurrences in Cather's work, of playing with variations on allusions, images, objects, themes, and ideas, is noted by many Cather scholars. Bernice Slote says that "perhaps more than most artists she worked a single, intricate design in which elements changed names and language and form but always remained part of the body. Nothing in Cather's work is unrelated to the whole" (*AT* ix). Fairy-tale images and motifs are elements of Cather's basic design, and we find them throughout her entire body of work.

When Nellie Birdseye, who is the first-person narrator of Myra Hen-shawe's story, recalls walking past the Driscoll place as a child, after Myra Driscoll had eloped with Oswald Henshawe, she says, "I thought of the place as being under a spell, like the Sleeping Beauty's palace; it had been in a trance, or lain in its flowers like a beautiful corpse, ever since that winter night when Love went out of the gates and gave the dare to Fate" (17). Like Magruder's Martha and Jewett's Martha, Nellie is drawn to Myra Henshawe because of her romantic past. In the Myra stories, Nellie has lived vicariously throughout her childhood, encouraged by her equally romantic-minded Aunt Lydia. Nellie tells us that Myra and her elopement with Oswald Henshawe had been the subject of the only interesting stories told in her life in the small town of Parthia, Illinois. Clearly Nellie Birdseye, unlike Mrs. Ramsay in *Lucy Gayheart* and Mrs. Ringer in *Sapphira and the Slave Girl,* was not "born interested."

We see in Nellie Birdseye a child fixated upon a romantic episode, one which she herself equates with fairy tales, specifically with "The Sleeping Beauty," although the reference to the beautiful corpse also recalls "Snow White." The name "Birdseye" itself implies a narrowly limited vision, while Nellie is a nickname for Helen. The most famous Helen was, of course, Helen of Troy, in Hellenic myth the world's most beautiful woman, and the quintessential example of woman as object. Helen was Paris's bribe for awarding Aphrodite the golden apple designating her the most beautiful of the goddesses, an event which led directly to the Trojan War. Here we have yet another situation in which "the eternal fact of sex is at the bottom of everything," and in which the jealousy between two women fires the action. Helen, too, was both princess and queen; she belongs in the same category of female as passive symbol of beauty and perfection as the Sleeping Beauty and Snow White.

In a myth that predates the generally accepted Hellenic version, Helen of Troy was an incarnation of the virgin moon goddess, the daughter of Hecuba, who embodies the crone and represents the dark side of the moon. Nellie our narrator uses moon imagery throughout; indeed, Myra slips an arm through Nellie's and calls her "moon-struck" (26), a term which in antiquity meant chosen by the moon goddess. One of the names for Hecuba is the Greek *Moerae,* a name which closely resembles Myra. Nellie and Myra, viewed in this manner, thus suggest daughter and mother, virgin and crone, princess and witch—two aspects of the same figure.

Here we should take a closer look at the two fairy tales to which Cather alludes. Why did she select these two tales in particular? What kind of tales are these? How are they alike? What does the allusion to these two tales say about the first-person narrator of this novel? What bearing do they have on the outcome?

Both "The Sleeping Beauty" and "Snow White" are first of all initiation stories, addressing the rite of passage translating an adolescent girl into adulthood. In both stories the initiate falls into a deathlike sleep, to awaken only when ready to assume adulthood, which promises marriage to a prince and the inheritance of a kingdom. Max Lüthi says that the princess in stories like this is an image of the human spirit: the story portrays the endowment, peril, paralysis, and redemption not of just one girl, but of all mankind. The soul of man again and again suffers convulsions and paralysis, and each time—with luck—it can be revived, healed, redeemed. With luck! The abnormal individual, of course, can also remain in the paralysed condition, unable to rediscover the fountainhead of life in himself and to re-establish contact with his surroundings. (*LO* 24)

The fairy tale promises that "a new, larger life is to come after the deathlike sleep—that after the isolation, a new form of contact and community will follow" (*LO* 24).

According to Bruno Bettelheim, "'The Sleeping Beauty' emphasizes the long quiet concentration on oneself that is . . . needed" (*B* 225) in the process of finding oneself in the transition between childhood and adulthood, a statement which can also be made for "Snow White." Finding oneself, for both Lüthi and Bettelheim, involves making a human connection, symbolized by the prince's kiss, which signals reentry into the human community. The lesson to be learned is that only by establishing a human bond can one live happily ever after.

This adolescent sleep also symbolizes the human dream and longing for "everlasting youth and perfection" (*B* 234). The Sleeping Beauty in her time-arrested kingdom and Snow White in her glass coffin recall Keats's "still unravished bride of quietness," a source of inspiration for so much fine literature, including *The Great Gatsby, Sartoris,* and *All the King's Men,* novels whose authors all owe debts to Willa Cather. All contain manifestations of this same archetype. The danger of this sleep is that the sleeper, fearing change and the "awful responsibility of Time," will fail to wake up. "During their sleep the heroine's beauty is a frigid one; theirs is the isolation of narcissism. In such self-involvement which excludes the rest of the world there is no suffering, but also no knowledge to be gained, no feelings to be experienced" (*B* 234). One should note, however, that males as well as females fall prey to the Sleeping Beauty syndrome, as Warren illustrates so convincingly with Jack Burden in *All the King's Men.* The moral of both "The Sleeping Beauty" and "Snow White," which Burden discovers so traumatically, is the necessity of awakening to life.

In addition, both fairy tales are considered nature myths, with the sleeping princess symbolizing winter and her awakening the coming of spring, or resurrection. "The Sleeping Beauty," especially, is an ancient nature myth, derived according to Frazer's *Golden Bough* from the basic vegetation myth of the corn god, and classified by Mircea Eliade as a "myth of the eternal return." Readers expect both death and resurrection when they read "The Sleeping Beauty" and "Snow White"; they accept death because they know resurrection follows. Willa Cather has had resurrection myths on her mind before. Alexandra in *O Pioneers!* becomes part of the land and is given "out again in the yellow wheat, in the

Figure 3. Sleeping Beauty and the Prince

"The Sleeping Beauty" suggests that a long period of quiet concentration on oneself is necessary in the transition between childhood and adulthood. Nellie Birdseye prolongs this period. She is finally awakened not by the prince's kiss, but rather by Myra's death.

(Illustration by Gustave Doré, from Perrault's Fairy Tales)

Figure 4. Snowdrop in the Coffin
Snow White's deathlike sleep symbolizes the human dream
and longing for everlasting youth and recalls Keats's "still
unravished bride of quietness."
(Illustration by Lancelot Speed, from The Red Fairy Book, *ed.*
Andrew Lang, published by Longmans, Green and Co.,
London, 1899; Dover edition, 1966)

rustling corn, in the shining eyes of youth!" (309), lines which resonate with Whitman as well as with the myth of Osiris, the Egyptian vegetation god who was buried in token each spring to give life to the earth.

Both Myra and Nellie embody many of the ingredients of fairy tale. Myra, like most fairy-tale princesses, is an orphan, raised and doted upon by a great uncle who functions as her father-king. Like a princess, Myra lives in "great splendor" (12) in a large stone house within a park, surrounded by a high iron fence. She is given jewels and gowns, a splendid riding horse and a fine piano on which to exercise her princessly musical skills. She is feted with balls and garden parties among the apple trees, with her own silver-instrumented band to play for her. When of age, she falls in love with a handsome and promising young man, a poor student who is the son of a schoolmaster. Her father-surrogate disapproves of the match, and so they elope in great style, with all the town waiting to see the couple come arm in arm out of the big iron gates to drive away in a sleigh.

In a true fairy tale, the princess's betrothed would have won the king's favor with some courageous, kingdom-saving deed, the two would have become the inheritors of the kingdom, and all would have lived happily ever after. Or using another typical fairy-tale plot, one more common for a male protagonist, Myra, as a fairy-tale hero who leaves home because of a family conflict, such as Myra's with her uncle over Oswald, would set out on a journey into the world, where she would encounter challenges and adventures and eventually win fame, fortune, and reconciliation with her father. Instead, Myra, disinherited permanently by her uncle, finds ordinary dailiness, a mundane life in which she has "to take account of shirts and railway trains, and getting a double chin in the bargain" (19). Aunt Lydia's response to Nellie's oft-asked question is that Myra and Oswald, Nellie's fairy-tale prince and princess, were only as "happy as most people" (17). Rather than living happily ever after, Nellie's desired denouement, the Henshawes signal early on that Nellie's fairy-tale vision is flawed.

Nellie tells us that she was fifteen when she first met Myra Henshawe. Myra also makes the point of saying to Nellie during this first meeting, "And you must be fifteen now, by my mournful arithmetic—am I right?" (6). This text makes significant the fact of Nellie's age. The Sleeping Beauty in the Grimm brothers' tale is specifically "in her fifteenth year" (*G* 177) when she opens the door into a room, sees the evil thirteenth fairy spinning flax, takes the spindle which pricks her hand, and falls into a hundred-year sleep from which she will awaken into sexual maturity. Bettelheim tells us that in the past, "fifteen was often the age at which menstruation began" (*B* 232). Fifteen, too, was a magic age for Willa Cather, and many of her characters make the transition from childhood to adulthood at this age. Nellie's age is so important that the novel's first sentence is, "I first met Myra Henshawe when I was fifteen" (3).

Both Nellie and the Sleeping Beauty, fifteen-year-old girls on the threshold of adulthood, look into a room and see at the end a single female figure who will trigger their entry into the adult world. For the Sleeping Beauty, this figure is the thirteenth fairy, who holds the forbidden spindle, an accepted phallic symbol. According to Bettelheim,

> The thirteen fairies in the Brothers Grimm's story are reminiscent of the thirteen lunar months into which the year was once, in ancient times, divided. . . . [M]enstruation typically occurs with the twenty-eight-day cycle frequency of lunar months, and not with the twelve months which our year is divided into. Thus, the number of twelve good fairies plus a thirteenth evil one indicates symbolically that the fatal 'curse' refers to menstruation. (*B* 232)

Menstruation signals the end of a female's childhood. Bettelheim's interpretation is certainly plausible.

Assuming, however, the thirteen fairies suggest the thirteen lunar months, then the moon itself traditionally symbolizes birth, death, and rebirth—the inevitable cycle. The statement that "the fatal 'curse' refers to menstruation" has an offensive ring, suggesting, since the tale is a universal one, told to and applying to females and males alike, that the female is responsible for the end of human childhood. In a recent translation of Perrault's "Sleeping Beauty," the thirteenth fairy is called the *old* fairy instead of the *evil* fairy.[1] The implication here is just slightly different, suggesting the inevitability of aging and death in human life with less sinister and sexist undertones.

For Nellie Birdseye, this same figure at the end of the room is Myra Henshawe, who sits holding a guitar, a womb-like object rather than a phallic one, but perhaps having the same symbolic implication as the spindle. Readers have been puzzled by this guitar of Cousin Bert's which Myra is softly playing when Nellie first meets her, a curiously extraneous detail without some specifically symbolic purpose. Interpreting the guitar as counterpart to the Sleeping Beauty's spindle is a satisfactory answer to this riddle. And Nellie's childhood is over when she first encounters Myra Henshawe with her guitar as certainly as it is for the Sleeping Beauty with the thirteenth fairy and her spindle.

At this very early point in the novel, we are already wondering who our princess is, Myra or Nellie? The answer, of course, is both. In Jung's symbolic interpretation of fairy tales, various figures represent aspects of the same person. If we use fairy tale to explicate this complex novel, then Nellie and Myra are two forms of the same person, doubles of the same life at different stages.

If we equate Nellie's first glimpse of Myra with the presence of the ominous thirteenth fairy, we must then address the sinister, or at least negative, aspects of Nellie's first perception of Myra. Firstly, Nellie perceives Myra, who up until this first meeting has been her fairy-tale princess, as a short, plump forty-five-year-old [a number which, interestingly, is three times fifteen] woman, dressed in black, with hair like the fleece of a Persian goat, who holds her head high to conceal her double chin—not a flattering picture. Myra is haughty and condescending to Nellie, who has been "overpraised" (7) to her. Both rude and insulting, Myra tells her that her solemnity is tiresome and then asks Nellie, who stares at Myra's amethyst necklace in embarrassment, whether the necklace annoys her. Nellie feels "overpowered by her—and stupid, hopelessly clumsy and stupid" (6). We are reminded here of those fairy tales in which the hero "appears as a dumbbell or a . . . Cinderella, as underestimated, despised, or disadvantaged" (*LF* 136). Nellie later tells us that stupidity made Myra laugh, "a terrible, angry laugh," with "a spark of zest and wild humor in it" (10), a laugh which made Nellie shiver, and which the reader construes to be in every way a witch-like laugh. In addition, Nellie assumes that Myra, in looking, is "estimating me" (6). All the evidence here points to an older woman who feels threatened by a younger one. And in the first pages of the novel we have one of the twists that occur throughout: Myra, Nellie's fairy-tale princess, has become more like her opposite, a witch, while Nellie plays the princess role.

Nellie has other attributes of a fairy-tale princess. The fairy-tale hero is almost always isolated—if not an orphan, then an only child, the youngest child, or a stepchild. Nellie, who is her mother's only daughter, "thought my mother scarcely appreciated me" (4), and both Myra and Aunt Lydia act as her fairy godmothers; Myra also acts as a kind of wicked stepmother. Like most fairy-tale princesses, Nellie is "passive,[2] obedient, self-sacrificing, hard-working, patient, and straight-laced" (Z 57). One might assume in her adoration of Myra Henshawe and her lifestyle that her own goal is "wealth, jewels, and a man to protect her property rights" (Z 57). And in fairy tale the moon is often an ally of the princess, sometimes providing her with wonderful gifts, such as Cinderella's dress of moonbeams in one version of the tale, for example. Nellie tells us more than once that Oswald has eyes "exactly like half-moons" (8); she takes careful note of the Saint Gaudens statue of Diana the moon goddess in Madison Square Garden; the Casta Diva aria from *Norma,* sung in a moonlit room, sounds to Nellie like "the quivering of moonbeams on the water" (47). Cather consistently establishes Nellie's association with the moon. One of the tensions Cather creates here is between Nellie's fixation on images of permanence—Sleeping Beauty's palace and Snow White's coffin—and her repeated association with the moon, an image of birth, death, and rebirth.

Here we must address Cather's veiled reference to "Snow White" in the phrase "lain in its flowers like a beautiful corpse, ever since that winter night when Love went out of the gates and gave the dare to Fate" (17), since both tales become entwined. Max Lüthi reminds us that "Snow White," in addition to being an initiation story, is also a tale of jealousy, as well as one dealing with the conflict of generations which occurs when an old order is being transferred to a new. The jealousy between Nellie and Myra is clearly set up from the beginning; indeed, it is a pattern which can be traced throughout this novel.

Furthermore, Myra's first glimpse of Nellie is in a mirror. One cannot imagine Cather setting up a situation like this one and alluding to "Snow White" within a few pages without having clear intentions. Fairy-tale readers recall the beautiful but aging queen who looks into her mirror and asks "Mirror, mirror, on the wall. Who is the fairest of us all?" Snow White's reflection eventually appears, while the mirror answers, "Queen, you are full fair, 'tis true, / But Snow White fairer is than you." Similarly, aging Myra looks into a mirror and sees the young woman who will replace her—at least as our narrator Nellie sees it.

As well as a tale of jealousy, "Snow White" is a story that addresses the conflict of generations when the power shifts from age to youth. We recall here Shakespeare's *King Lear,* another tale of the old order's passing, and one which is woven into the end of *My Mortal Enemy.* At the end of her life, Myra goes to die on a headland facing the sea, on what she refers to as "Gloucester's cliff," from Shakespeare's *Lear. King Lear,* too, like "The Sleeping Beauty" and "Snow White," is a kind of resurrection story, since Gloucester seeks the cliff to die and instead is saved by his son Edgar. *King Lear* is based on the old English fairy tale about a king whose favorite daughter, when asked how much she loved her father, replied, "As much as I love salt," and thus was banished from the kingdom.[3] Willa Cather is in excellent company in her use of fairy tales in her work. She says in *Not Under Forty,* "What we most love is . . . to have the old story brought home to us closer than ever before, enriched by all that the right man could draw from it and, by sympathetic insight, put into it. Shakespeare knew this fact very well, and the Greek dramatists long before him" (43). Cather is entirely conscious of her use of the old stories in this novel.

Bettelheim refers to fairy tales as a "metaphor by which we refer to a particular emotional constellation within the family" (195), a constellation which is most often a triad. One of the ways to read this complex novel is as such a fairy-tale triad. Nellie and Myra then represent a mother and daughter who each want the attentions of a male, Oswald, who represents the father. Thus Myra becomes the aging mother/queen, Oswald the father/king, and Nellie the daughter/princess. Consistent with this particular fairy-tale triad, Oswald as father/king is a weak individual; the dynamic is created by the mother/daughter. In the first pages of the novel, not only is the jealousy between Myra and Nellie clearly established, but also Nellie's positive feelings for Oswald, whom she perceives as emitting "personal bravery, magnanimity, and a fine way of doing things" (8), kingly qualities all. Nellie, along with Aunt Lydia, sides with Oswald throughout.

Reading *My Mortal Enemy* with "The Sleeping Beauty" and "Snow White"

Figure 5.   The Queen Looking in the Mirror
The mirror motif is found in both *The Song of the Lark* and *My Mortal Enemy*.
(Illustration by Lancelot Speed, from The Red Fairy Book, *ed. Andrew Lang, published by Longmans, Green and Co., London, 1899; Dover edition, 1966)*

as a kind of substructure results in a new conclusion as to the identity of the enemy of the title. On her deathbed, Myra, overheard by Oswald and Nellie, says, "I have been true in friendship; I have faithfully nursed others in sickness. . . . Why must I die like this, alone with my mortal enemy?" (95). If Nellie is the princess, who on the death of the aging queen will marry the king and inherit the kingdom, then Nellie may be Myra's "mortal enemy." Perhaps Myra recognized her usurper when she first saw Nellie's reflection in the mirror in Aunt Lydia's parlor. This conclusion is supported to some extent by Judith Fryer's recent study, which asserts that *time* is Myra Henshawe's mortal enemy. Fryer illustrates her conclusion with a quotation from Simone Weil: "[I]t is because man's love has been for her body . . . that woman's 'most mortal enemy then is time—time our torture'" (385). If a female's only source of fulfillment is through males, as is the case with Nellie and Myra, as well as with the Sleeping Beauty, Snow White, and Helen of Troy, then time, which ages the body and causes a male to turn to a younger woman, is indeed her enemy.

But taking this argument one step further, perhaps it is romantic love itself, symbolized by the prince and princess of fairy tales, romantic love with its temporality and false illusions, which is Myra Henshawe's mortal enemy. Equipped with enough passion to make her seem to Father Fay like one of the early martyrs of the Church, and with "enough desperate courage for a regiment" (76), Myra nonetheless spent all her energy, her life's force, on romance. At the end of her life she is alone with the two people who symbolize this romantic love—Oswald, her own object of romance and sexual passion, and Nellie Birdseye, who will carry the vision. She is indeed alone with her mortal enemy, and the multiple ironies of this term reverberate. At the end Myra is unequipped because of that enemy to face the greatest mystery of life—her own death.

Willa Cather finished *My Mortal Enemy* and immediately began writing *Death Comes for the Archbishop,* a book about a spirit which continues to expand and grow until upon his deathbed the Archbishop sits "in the middle of his own consciousness" (290), his own quiet center. Cather leaps from the most bitter of deaths, Myra Henshawe's, whose lifetime focus on romantic love has denied her spiritual growth, to the Archbishop's, whose life is so well-lived that death is its reward. And we have yet again another Catherian recurrence, to use Bernice Slote's phrase—beware of spending creative energy, true passion, on a traditional love relationship—a theme woven throughout Cather's fiction, symbolized in this novel by a fairy tale. Sharon O'Brien argues that Cather often reverses male-authored narratives with culturally defined gender roles. Here she is playing with just such a reversal, using in fairy tales a form in which gender roles are rigid and inflexible, and twisting them ironically.

At this point we should take a closer look at another possible meaning in this novel. In both "The Sleeping Beauty" and "Snow White," the female protagonist can find release from imprisonment and self-fulfillment only through males. Myra, too, expects to find the meaning for her own life through romance. Her middle years are spent as a kind of matchmaker, an Aunt Lydia herself, who takes vicarious pleasure in the love affairs of her younger friends, even though she insists, "I hate old women who egg on courtships" (29). Nellie, on the other hand, remains in a kind of narcissistic trance, waiting for her prince to awaken her. Perhaps Cather's point is an ironic one here, a feminist view, suggesting that both Nellie and Myra should have stopped identifying themselves through males and looked for some meaning in life beyond romantic attachments. The women artists in the novel stand in telling contrast to Nellie and Myra, especially Madame Modjeska, whose beautifully modelled hands reveal a "nobler worldliness . . . hands to hold a sceptre, or a chalice—or by courtesy, a sword" (46), all symbols of maximal individual power, the last a symbol of male power.

In his feminist criticism of fairy tales, Jack Zipes says, "[F]airy tales operate ideologically to indoctrinate children so that they will conform to dominant social standards which are not necessarily established in their behalf" (Z 18). Willa Cather rebelled throughout her life against stereotypic female roles; although her pleasure in fairy tales is apparent in her work, she must have been aware of this negative dimension. The contradictory legacy of fairy tales is the elegance of the tales themselves and the lesson they teach of female submissiveness and passivity. Jennifer Waelti-Walters in *Fairy Tales and the Female Imagination* says, "Nobody in her right mind could possibly want to be a fairy tale princess. . . . She is a totally powerless prisoner, in turn the victim of circumstance, of an older woman and of men of all ages" (1). Perhaps this statement illustrates one of Cather's points in this puzzling novel, as it may also apply to her portrayal of Marian Forrester in *A Lost Lady,* another fairy-tale princess who can find her own identity only through males.[4] Yet again is Willa Cather a writer far ahead of her time, since not until the 1970s did feminist readings of fairy tales begin to appear.

Romance has been the focus of Myra Henshawe's life, the object of all the intensity of her passionate nature, her "idolatry." And "violent natures like hers sometimes turn against themselves . . . against themselves and all their idolatries" (96), much like the witch who furiously dances herself to death in red-hot shoes at Snow White's wedding. In "real" life, time and the realities of aging and death inevitably destroy such narrowly defined romance. Lover/prince becomes nurse, as Oswald nurses Myra while she bitterly rebukes him for it, saying, "It's bitter enough that I should have to take service from you—you whom I have loved so well" (92). Myra, at the end of her life, has failed to grow spiritually, and has not prepared herself to face life's mysteries. She confesses to Nellie that she has always been "a greedy, selfish, and worldly woman," who "wanted success and a place in the world" (78). When Myra realizes her death is near and how unprepared she is to meet it, she makes several desperate attempts to understand the ultimate mysteries.

In addition to a priest, Myra consults a fortune-teller, grasping at both sacred and profane, Christian and pagan for answers. If we assume the fortune-teller used the Tarot deck to read Myra's fortune, a reasonable assumption, we might then use these cards as another key to the secrets of this novel, not unrelated to fairy tales, since the Tarot deck revolves around many of the same figures and archetypes as fairy tales. If Cather had probed into Catholicism in the Middle Ages, as Edith Lewis informs us she did long before she came to write *Death Comes for the Archbishop,* then she would surely have come across the Tarot cards, linked as they are with the history of the Catholic Church.

When Nellie runs into the Henshawes in the crumbling boarding house in California after a lapse of ten years, Myra tells Nellie she knew Nellie would come because "a wise woman has been coming to read my fortune for me, and the queen of hearts has been coming up out of the pack when she had no business to; a beloved friend coming out of the past" (62). In the Tarot deck, from which the modern one is derived, this card, called the Queen of Cups, represents Virginal, the virgin form of the tripartite goddess who rules fate, called by the Greeks *Moerae,* that name which is so close to Myra. This virgin goddess, described as "glacial and remote" (*W* 160), lives in a "lofty ice cave among the clouds in the realm of eternal snow" (160). She is associated with "water in all its forms: cold, crystalline, perfect, untouchable" (160). Associating Nellie with Virginal helps to explain the snow imagery connected with her throughout the novel—for example, her snow-blurred vision, or her perception of winter "like a polar bear led on a leash by a beautiful woman" (25).

In addition, Helen of Troy is considered one of the incarnations of Virginal, in turn one form of the triple goddess. Thus perhaps we hear further notes in the chord Cather strikes when she chooses the name "Nellie." Further yet, the Sleeping Beauty and Snow White both represent this form of the triple goddess. The virgin and the princess are closely connected in the history of mythology, the second deriving from the first. Western Medieval poets referred to this figure as "Virginal the Ice Queen," while German minstrels sang of Virginal's descent to the lowlands to marry a German prince, an interesting detail since Oswald's mother was German. Virginal wearied of her prince, however, and returned to her ice cave, remaining forever inaccessible to males. Virginal was the inspiration for Hans Christian Andersen's fairy tale "The Snow Queen." Too many associations can be made between Nellie and Virginal to assume coincidence, especially since the text itself links Nellie to the Queen of Hearts.

Furthermore, the Irish version of "Myra" is "Moira," a name derived from the Greek *Moerae,* meaning fate. Since Myra is herself Irish, as we are reminded more than once, perhaps we can assume Cather is suggesting this connection between Myra and fate. We recall here Nellie's statement that when

QUEEN of CUPS.

Figure 6.   Queen of Cups Tarot Card
(Illustration from page 201 of The Pictorial Key
to the Tarot *by Arthur Edward Waite. Copyright
© 1971 by Rudolf Steiner Publications.
Reprinted by permission of Harper and Row,
Publishers, Inc.)*

Myra walked out of the gates of the Driscoll place carrying only her muff and her port-monnaie,[5] she "gave the dare to Fate" (17). In the Tarot deck the card called the Wheel of Fortune is represented by Fortuna, yet another name for this triple goddess ruling fate. The first form of Fortuna is the virgin; the second the nurturing, sustaining mother; and the third the destroying crone.

We see Myra Henshawe in three distinct and separate periods of her life in *My Mortal Enemy:* Myra the princess as Nellie first remembers her, embodies the virgin form; Myra in her middle years, when Nellie first meets her, represents the sustaining and nurturing mother, or the queen. Indeed, she serves as a mother to Nellie and most of her friends. The form which Myra takes in the final section of the novel is the third form of Fortuna—the destroying crone, the witch of fairy tale. Interestingly, the primary symbol of Fortuna, the goddess of the wheel who rules time and fate, is the moon. Again we are reminded of the moon imagery used by Nellie, especially in connection with Oswald. Oswald himself, in Myra's fortune, might be connected with the fool, or joker, the man made foolish by the moon, called in medieval European carnivals "the Prince of Love." Oswald, like the fool in the Tarot deck, seems to learn nothing in his journey through life; he is as unenlightened at the end as the beginning, still chasing after young women. When Myra dies, Oswald goes to Alaska, perhaps in search of another Virginal in her ice world, to begin the cycle again.

Nellie, although she is twenty-five at the end of the novel, is as colorless, devoid of personality, lacking in self-definition, as passive and docile as any Grimm brothers' fifteen-year-old princess. She still remains frozen in a kind of Snow White/Sleeping Beauty self-absorption, waiting for her prince, as inaccessible as Virginal. On Myra's death, instead of awakening Nellie to life, Oswald leaves for Alaska. Nellie is left with only Myra's jewels—not a prince and a kingdom, but only the promised amethysts to remind her that she cannot freeze herself forever young in time, but she, too, will age and die like Myra. In the next novel, the Archbishop rubs Father Joseph's amethyst ring, left to him after Joseph's death, to get a sense of warmth and connection. In this novel, Myra's amethysts remind Nellie of her friend's life, and of her death, and they chill her heart.

Nellie Birdseye's most basic problem is her terror of death. In fairy tales people neither age nor die, but live happily ever after. Nellie's favorite tales, too, promise resurrection. And one of her namesakes, Helen of Troy, daughter of Zeus and Leda in Hellenic mythology, was immortal. Perhaps Nellie's fear of death makes her insist that Myra lived to see the dawn. Terrified of death, Nellie tries to remain in a state of adolescent sleep, as colorless as a rabbit who remains still under the hunter's gun, pretending to be part of the landscape. Because of her own terror of death, Nellie thinks that Myra's uncle "had got, after all, the more romantic part" (19): he appeared to Nellie to be received into the church without experiencing the dark night of the soul, or "the end of all flesh" (19). On the contrary, Nellie lives with Myra through her dark night and watches her experience the excruciating demise and disintegration of the flesh, her own ultimate terror. Cather may be articulating here her own fear of aging and death, which her biographers report, and her awareness of the futility of her own longing to hide in a childhood world.

At the conclusion of *My Mortal Enemy* all these entwined allusions to tales and Tarot cards become one. In her crone or witch form, Myra sees the dawn because all ancient tales and holy rites promise resurrection. The crone becomes again the virgin, the Sleeping Beauty always awakes as winter gives way to spring, as the eternal cycle repeats itself. Nellie feels a chill around her heart because she knows, dawn-sighted or not, Myra died. She also knows that one day she will take Myra's place as dying crone. And she understands at the end the limitations of her own romantic, fairy-tale vision—Nellie's reason, after all, for telling Myra's tale. Romantic love is Nellie Birdseye's idolatry, too, and unless she expands her vision to encompass greater mysteries, it will be her "mortal enemy" as well.

Once the extent to which fairy tale shapes this novel is made clear, it is then difficult to believe Cather's use was not part of her basic plan. If Nellie Birdseye's fairy-tale vision is her "mortal enemy," then fairy tale lies at the novel's very heart. In the next novel, *Death Comes for the Archbishop,* Cather's use is much less apparent, less strategic, but equally as pervasive.

4

From Legend to Fairy Tale
in *Death Comes for the Archbishop*

James Woodress says of Willa Cather's *Death Comes for the Archbishop* that "the more one examines this novel, the more echoes and reverberations and hidden art one finds in it" (224). In fact, one is hard-pressed to find a major Cather critic who does not comment upon these multiple undertones woven through all Cather's work. Woodress suggests *The Divine Comedy* and *Pilgrim's Progress* as Cather's most significant literary influences for *Archbishop*, aside from the medieval *Golden Legend* which she herself cites.

But one of the still-hidden arts playing beneath the surfaces of *Archbishop* is the age-old art of fairy tales. Perhaps it is impossible to work around texts like *The Divine Comedy, Pilgrim's Progress,* and *The Golden Legend* without echoing fairy tales, since the same archetypal patterns are predominant in all. Nonetheless, all of Cather's work is so replete with fairy-tale allusions and motifs that one can argue that their part in her psychological makeup conditioned her way of looking at the world, and thus are part of the most basic fabric of her work.

In the novel which precedes *Archbishop, My Mortal Enemy,* and the one which immediately follows it, *Shadows on the Rock,* fairy tale plays a crucial part. One cannot begin to fully understand these novels without considering Cather's conscious use of fairy tale within them. Since these two novels show her mind clearly working with these forms during this period in her life, we should look at the way in which fairy tale functions in this novel that she wrote in between, and note its relationship to legend, with which we know Cather was working in *Archbishop.*

Cather writes in a letter to *The Commonweal* an explanation of the genesis of *Death Comes for the Archbishop:*

> My book was a conjunction of the general and the particular, like most works of the imagination. I had all my life wanted to do something in the style of legend, which is absolutely the reverse of dramatic treatment. Since I first saw the Puvis de Chavannes frescoes of the life

of Saint Genevieve in my student days, I have wished that I could try something a little like that in prose; something without accent, with none of the artificial elements of composition. In the Golden Legend the martyrdoms of the saints are no more dwelt upon than are the trivial incidents of their lives; it is as though all human experiences, measured against one supreme spiritual experience, were of about the same importance. The essence of such writing is not to hold the note, not to use an incident for all there is in it—but to touch and pass on. I felt that such writing would be a kind of discipline in these days when the "situation" is made to count for so much in writing, when the general tendency is to force things up. In this kind of writing the mood is the thing—all the little figures and stories are mere improvisations that come out of it. (*OW* 9, 10)

The Golden Legend, or *Legenda Aurea,* to which Cather refers here was written by Jacobus de Voragine between 1243 and 1273, and is the single most important collection of medieval saints' legends. Originally written in Latin, it was translated into English by Caxton in 1483, and then printed and published in an exquisite illustrated edition by William Morris in 1892. It was probably this edition which inspired Cather.

It is fascinating to note that Jacobus de Voragine, a wise, gentle, scholarly man like Cather's Latour, later became the archbishop of Genoa. He was canonized by Pope Pius VII in 1816, and thus his own life is itself a saint's life. We note, too, that the word *legenda* originally meant "that which is to be read"; and whatever was written down to be read in this early period was executed by clerics.[1] How very interesting that Cather has chosen two clerics for the protagonists of her narrative suggested by the *Golden Legend,* one of them an archbishop.

In a sense, *Archbishop* can be read as a series of stories collected by the two priests: in almost every instance Latour and Vaillant either participate in the material of legend, or they listen themselves to tales of various types being told. Many of these stories are actual legends of the countryside. Although Father Jesus of Isleta tells Latour the legend of Fray Baltazar, the story of the corpulent priest who was thrown from the rock at Acoma was one known in Santa Fé long before Willa Cather incorporated it into her novel. The story of Father Martinez and Father Lucero also belonged to Santa Fé before it found itself in Cather's novel, although Latour and Vaillant become part of the cast.

Father Joseph tells Latour the story of the silver-toned bell found in the basement of San Miguel in which Latour can hear the sound of Moorish silver; Padre Herrera tells the two priests the legend of the Virgin of Guadaloupe; Father Joseph is one of the players in the story of the white mules, a tale containing typical elements of Southwestern humor;[2] both priests take part in the tale of wayside murderer Buck Scales, an old motif of legend and fairy tale which Robert Penn Warren uses for a stunning episode in his poem "Audubon." These are examples of the way in which the priests and the stories are woven together: as Cather puts it in her letter, "a conjunction of the general and the particular."

Latour, particularly, becomes the repository of stories much as Cécile does in the next novel, *Shadows on the Rock*. Latour is initially appointed by the Vatican to the vast and unwieldy diocese in New Mexico because he is French, and "they are the great organizers" (9). Cather's archbishop not only organizes the Catholic diocese in New Mexico, but serves also as the organizing agent behind the stories that make up the narrative as well. Thus *The Golden Legend*,[3] a series of stories collected by an archbishop, influenced Cather's novel in its most basic structure as well as in its more general form and in mood and tone.

According to folklorist Max Lüthi, legends and fairy tales are closely related, overlapping forms. It's impossible to work with either without involving the other. Although saints' legends were originally written to be read, they soon became part of an oral tradition along with local legends and fairy tales. Saints' and local legends, unlike fairy tales, are at least partly true; the original teller of a legend believed the tale. Behind a legend's author, however, "is a hidden 'author' anonymous and manifold, whose memory stretches back through generations" (*GL* x)—from the group memory, or collective unconscious.

All legendary heroes, like saints and princes, have common characteristics: "He must have all the virtues . . . must work all imaginable wonders, out do the greatest magicians in magic, conquer the power of the Devil himself. He must be the master of Nature, able to dominate the fiercest beasts, and to command the winds and the sea" (*GL* x). Heroes of legends, like heroes of fairy tale, are types rather than individuals, and represent absolutes; just as princes are absolutely noble, saints are absolutely unblemished, and both princesses and virgins are absolutely pure.

While fairy tales are diffused throughout many cultures, legends are confined to one place and are slow to migrate. Place and time details are often specific, as opposed to "once upon a time in a faraway kingdom." Cather adheres strictly to the form of saints' legend, for example, when she writes in Padre Herrera's telling of the story of Our Lady of Guadalupe: "On Saturday, December 9th, in the year 1531, a poor neophyte of the monastery of St. James was hurrying down Tapeyac hill to attend Mass in the City of Mexico" (47). After grounding her reader in "real" details, she then tells us that the Holy Mother dressed in blue and gold appeared on the road and called the tale's teller by name. Interestingly, this is a favorite Cather opening. The first chapter of *Archbishop*, a book which Stouck asserts is itself a saints' legend, opens: "One afternoon in the autumn of 1851 a solitary horseman, followed by a pack-mule, was pushing through an arid stretch of country somewhere in central New Mexico" (17). Similarly, *Shadows* begins: "One afternoon late in October of the year 1697, Euclide Auclair, the philosopher apothecary of Quebec, stood on the top of Cap Diamant gazing down the broad, empty river far beneath him" (3). Cather uses this kind of specificity for the same purpose—to make the fantastic seem more believable, and the distant more immediate. And this opening is yet another way of saying, "Once upon a time."

Perhaps the most interesting single characteristic of both legend and fairy tale for our purpose here is the extent to which both rely on miracle. Max Lüthi says of legend that its very core is miracle (37), that "the entire tale is told for the sake of this miracle" (41): the power of this miracle has a kind of "fascination of its own" (41). The major difference we note here is that in fairy tale the emphasis is not upon miracle, but rather on miracle's result. The miracle itself has no fascination at all, but is taken as a matter of course. Nonetheless, the outcome depends upon miracle.

One of the basic themes of *Archbishop* involves the nature of miracle, and the novel abounds with miracles of one kind and another. For example, the novel begins with a miracle—Latour's salvation in the desert after praying under the cruciform tree to the Virgin Mary. One of the first legends in this string of tales and legends is Father Herrera's recounting of the miraculous appearance of the Virgin of Guadaloupe, which is in every way a prototype of saints' legend. When Latour journeyed into Old Mexico to claim his diocese from the recalcitrant Bishop of Durango, he met on the way priests who "related many stories of the blessed experiences of the early Franciscan missionaries. Their way through the wilderness had blossomed with little miracles, it seemed" (279). The stories of Father Junipero are recounted here at the end of Cather's series, although Latour heard them at the beginning of his life. Father Junipero's story of the Holy Family is one of the most significant of the collection, reiterating once again Cather's theme of "greatness returning to simplicity" (282), like an El Greco or a Latour in New Mexico.[4]

Cather's basic story, which holds legends and tales together, is the story of Latour and Vaillant; it is based, as she tells us, on the real lives of Lamy and Macheboeuf, found in William Howlett's *The Life of the Right Reverend Joseph P. Macheboeuf*. Although founded upon historical figures and biographical facts, Cather's rendering of the story of Latour and Vaillant contains archetypal patterns. David Stouck says that the novel's primary archetypal pattern is the Christian life, "Christ's teaching, suffering, and martyrdom" (132), a paradigm for saints' legend. Perhaps, too, it is in her story of Latour and Vaillant, which Stouck suggests is modeled after the form of saints' legend, that Cather succeeds best in her attempt to tell a story without accent. The final effect is like that of a saints' legend—serene, composed, and without stress. It is like the Bayeux tapestry which runs along, yard after yard, with individual episodes woven together into a stunning whole.

An equally good case, however, can be made to establish that the ancient fairy-tale motif of the two brothers is the primary archetypal pattern of *Archbishop*. This motif, thought to be the germ of the oldest fairy tale in the world, was found in an Egyptian papyrus of about 1250 B.C. Many versions of this tale are in existence, but this oldest Egyptian version bears a marked similarity to *Archbishop*. In this ancient tale, a "happy resolution requires that the brothers free themselves of oedipal and sibling jealousy and support each other" (*B* 92).

The motif of the two brothers is as follows: two brothers who are in every way exact opposites set out together to make their fortunes in the world. On the way they meet helpers, most often in the form of magic animals; a magic tree with marvelous and mysterious powers; or they may encounter the spirit of a loving and nurturing mother of childhood who intervenes with magic powers. The brothers have adventures, meet with dangers, and eventually are separated. A magic object unites them in spirit, sometimes letting one of them know when the other is in danger. At the end they are reunited, and live thereafter happily. "What all these stories have in common are features which suggest the identity of the two heroes, one of whom is cautious and reasonable, but ready to risk his life to rescue the other brother, who foolishly exposes himself to terrible perils" (*B* 91). Readers of Cather's *Archbishop* readily see how her story of the two priests conforms to this age-old pattern.

Let us begin by considering our two priests. The two brothers in this tale "stand for seemingly incompatible aspects of the human personality" (*B* 90). And never were two characters more exactly opposites in every way than Latour and Vaillant. And, too, they are indeed brothers, fellow seminarians in the Jesuit order of the Catholic Church.

The Latours, firstly, "were an old family of scholars and professional men, while the Vaillants were people of a much humbler station in the provincial world" (224). While Joseph's father was a baker, Latour is described as the most princely of priests:

> His bowed head was not that of an ordinary man,—it was built for the seat of a fine intelligence. His brow was open, generous, reflective, his features handsome and somewhat severe. There was singular elegance about the hands below the fringed cuffs of the buckskin jacket. Everything showed him to be a man of gentle birth—brave, sensitive, courteous. His manners, even when he was alone in the desert, were distinguished. He had a kind of courtesy toward himself, toward his beasts, toward the juniper tree before which he knelt, and the God whom he was addressing. (19)

Vaillant is the peasant to Latour's prince, a kind of Sancho Panza to Latour's Don Quixote. He is short, skinny, and bowlegged, with tufts of white hair like dry hay, a blunt-tipped nose, thick lips, near-sighted eyes and a wart on his chin. We are told that "the Lord had made few uglier men" (37).

Latour is serene, aloof, deliberate, "much cooler and more critical in temper; hard to please, and often a little grey in mood" (225), while Vaillant is nervous, gregarious, rash, and "added a glow to whatever kind of human society he was dropped down into" (228). Latour excels in scholarship, Joseph in "the fervour of his faith" (226). Latour takes great pleasure in his few possessions—

beautiful books, Indian blankets, hand-embroidered linens, and hand-wrought silver—while Joseph has no possessions at all, except perhaps his mule Contento, and cared to have none. Vaillant loves the tamarisk tree because it was the tree of the people, found in front of the simplest adobe homes, while Latour loves the same tree for its shape and color. The difference between the two men is pointed up in their separate definitions of miracle: for Vaillant, a miracle is concrete, something you can hold in your hands and love. Latour's definition is abstract: "where there is great love there is always miracle" (50). At the end of their lives, Vaillant saves souls in the gold camps, while Latour builds a cathedral on a mountain of gold.

According to Bruno Bettelheim's psychological interpretation of fairy tales, one of the points of the tale of the two brothers is the need of each individual to integrate seemingly incompatible aspects of his or her personality. In other words, this is another divided-self tale, yet another example of what Bernice Slote refers to as a "fascinating Catherian recurrence" (*AB* 10). Cather's first novel, *Alexander's Bridge,* is a story about a divided self: both Thea Kronberg and Jack Burden are divided selves who search for integration, to mention only two. Here again, in *Archbishop* we are confronted with one of Willa Cather's major themes.

Cather's two brotherly priests representing all manner of opposites embark together from their hometown of Clermont in the province of Auvergne in France on a journey to New Mexico, a place described in mythic terms as so distant that as far as they could discern, "no one had ever been there" (21). It "lay in the middle of a dark continent" (21).[5] On their journey they have typical adventures, first nearly perishing in a shipwreck, losing all their possessions except for a few books which Latour saves at the risk of his life. Latour is then seriously injured when his wagon turns over. When they finally reach Santa Fé they separate, true to the two brothers motif, Vaillant remaining "at home" while Latour journeys even farther into the unknown to reclaim his vicarate from the Bishop of Durango in Old Mexico. Thus far, our story is remarkably similar to the fairy tale of the two brothers.

The first time we meet Jean Latour he is lost in a desert of ovens, analogous to the fantastic fairy-tale forest in which the hero is lost when he begins his journey. Indeed, this "forest" is personified much like the forest of fairy tale: "the hills thrust out of the ground so thickly that they seemed to be pushing each other, elbowing each other aside, tipping each other over" (18). Latour's situation is a match to the one of the following fairy-tale hero:

[T]he brother who leaves soon finds himself in a deep, dark forest, where he feels lost, having given up the organization of his life which the parental home provided, and not yet having built up the inner structures which we develop only under the impact of life experiences we have to master more or less on our own. Since ancient times the near-impenetrable forest in which we get lost has symbolized the dark, hidden, near-impenetrable world of our unconscious. If we have lost the framework which gave structure to our past life and must now find our own way to become ourselves, and have entered this wilderness with an as yet undeveloped personality, when we succeed in finding our way out we shall emerge with a much more highly developed humanity. (*B* 94)

This trial in the desert is in every way such a test for Latour; not only is his faith tested, but also his ability to cope with the extremities of topography and climate in this wild new land. Latour is as much out of place in this land as the lost El Greco painting of Saint Francis which is alluded to in the prologue. Latour, suffering from thirst and exhaustion, sees a juniper tree which takes on the form of a cross in his eyes. He kneels under it, prays to the Holy Mother, and soon thereafter his mules catch the scent of water. Here we have two of the most common "helpers" of a fairy-tale protagonist—a tree with miraculous powers, and a loving and deceased mother who intervenes with magic or miracle. In Perrault's tale of "Cinderella," Cinderella prays to her dead mother under a tree planted on her mother's grave and receives her dress for the Prince's ball. Cather's Archbishop conforms here to an age-old fairy-tale pattern.[6]

Another useful analogy here is the good witch who is one of the figures a fairy-tale hero often meets while lost in the forest. Bettelheim tells us she represents "the all-giving mother of our infancy" (*B* 94). He says further that "it is this hope of finding her somewhere which gives us the strength to leave home" (94). Interestingly, both of Cather's priests leave home to serve a mother—the Holy Mother. "Auspice Maria" appears on the frontispage of the novel, as well as on Vaillant's signet ring. When Latour and Vaillant part for the last time, Vaillant comforts himself by murmuring "Auspice Maria" when he turns his back forever on Santa Fé and on his friend. Latour comforts himself by thinking: "A life need not be cold, or devoid of grace in the worldly sense, if it were filled by Her who was all the graces; Virgin-daughter, Virgin-mother, girl of the people and Queen of Heaven: 'le rêve suprême de la chair.' The nursery tale could not vie with Her in simplicity" (256).

By leaving home Cather's priests remain secure forever in the care of such a nurturing mother, the Holy Mother. And She is "all-giving, all-satisfying, as long as he does not insist on doing things his way and remains symbiotically tied to her" (*B* 95). By leaving worldly mothers and families, Latour and Vaillant can remain forever tied to a kind of childhood mother in the Mother of Christ. Both Latour and Vaillant evade the separation anxiety which pervades the consciousness of children, and which sets the stage for many fairy tales. By becoming priests, they hold onto the mother eternally, throughout life and after death. Cather's biographers suggest she suffered from this kind of separation anxiety, particularly at this time in her life, when her parents were aging and ill and she herself was even more acutely aware of her own mortality. A thread throughout her work is this search for the mother, which she seems to satisfy in some metaphorical sense in *Archbishop* and in *Shadows on the Rock*.[7]

A fairy-tale motif familiar to all of us is that of a hero, lost in the forest, who comes upon a house deep in the woods. We recognize this motif in "Snow White," "Goldilocks," and "Hansel and Gretel," to cite only a few that come quickly to mind. Latour not only is aided by a magic tree and a "deceased mother," but he then comes upon the house of an old man, Benito, kept in perfect order by his housekeeping daughter. Here again are the echoes of fairy tale. Daughters who keep house for fathers or brothers—or dwarfs—abound in fairy tale. We find a classic example of this motif in Cécile Auclair in Cather's next novel, *Shadows on the Rock*. In another episode, Latour and Vaillant are again lost, this time on the road to Mora, and come again to a house, this time to the house of the degenerate murderer Buck Scales. Father Junipero is also lost and comes upon a mysterious little house which has disappeared when he returns to find it. Thus the motif is repeated in separate tales.

Magic animals abound in fairy tale. In the Grimms' story "The Two Brothers," the brothers on their journey spare the lives of several kinds of animals. In gratitude, each animal gives the brothers a pair of its own kind. When the brothers separate, each one takes a set of animals which remain faithful companions. Echoed here are the two ivory-colored mules of the novel, Angelica and Contento, who are intelligent, affectionate, and "look at me like Christians" (60), according to Vaillant. They often seem magic, leading their masters out of many a crisis. These mules are described as having coats the color of pearls, with tails clipped at the end "into the shape of bells" (60), magic-sounding mules, indeed. Like the animals in Grimms' "The Two Brothers," Angelica and Contento "work together and, through doing so repeatedly, help their masters escape great dangers. This shows once more in fairy-tale fashion that successful living requires the working together" (*B* 96). Joseph, like a brother in the Grimms' tale, finally takes the pair when he departs for Colorado.

At the end of their lives, Father Joseph's amethyst ring serves as the "magic" object which unites the spirits of the brothers. In the Grimms' tale, a knife stuck into a tree signals each brother about the other's well-being by the amount of rust on each side. We should note that Cather's symbol, rather than a sword, is a circle, signaling harmony and continuity, a female symbol rather than a male one.

After Joseph's death, Latour touches the ring, now on his own hand, and senses his friend's closeness. When Latour is dying, "the thumb of his right hand would sometimes gently touch a ring on his forefinger, an amethyst with an inscription cut upon it, *Auspice Maria,*—Father Vaillant's signet-ring; and then he was almost certainly thinking of Joseph; of their life together here, in this room . . . in Ohio beside the Great Lakes . . . as young men in Paris . . . as boys at Montferrand" (283). Like the two brothers of fairy tale, Latour and Vaillant are reunited at the end.

Bruno Bettelheim states that the classic fairy-tale ending "they lived happily ever after" does not imply eternal life, but rather "that which alone can take the sting out of the narrow limits of our time on this earth: forming a truly satisfying bond to another" (*B* 10). He continues: "The tales teach that when one has done this, one has reached the ultimate in emotional security of existence and permanence of relation available to man; and this alone can dissipate the fear of death" (*B* 11). Latour and Vaillant not only live happily ever after, bonded as they are by their love for one another and for the Holy Mother, but the reader might infer—or hope—they find eternal life as well, and perhaps together. The close of the novel is Archbishop Latour's death, when he cries again to his friend, "Allons! L'invitation du voyage!" (285). For Latour and Vaillant, the end is again the beginning.

James Woodress aptly calls *Death Comes for the Archbishop* a masterpiece of cultural assimilation. To focus on a single aspect is to neglect all the rest; to miss the whole of a work like this is to miss all. But fairy tales are a part, if a lesser and more subtly hidden one, of this cultural assimilation. To appreciate *Death Comes for the Archbishop,* Cather scholars must address all the cultural strains, and how they are woven together to create the whole. If Jacobus de Voragine's contribution in writing *The Golden Legend* was "that he gave to the people, in a fresh and gracious form, so much that they already knew and cherished" (*GL* xv), Willa Cather has succeeded in fashioning similar material not only into a fresh and gracious form, but into a magnificent and original work of art.

Cather has, at this point in her writing career, retold the Cinderella story with an ending in which the princess is not lost to marriage, but born to art. She has used fairy tale as visual perception—form, shape and color—in *My Ántonia;* as symbol in *My Mortal Enemy;* and as a primary archetypal pattern in *Death Comes for the Archbishop.* In her next novel, *Shadows on the Rock,* Cather combines these uses, and taps all her knowledge of fairy tale, to write a novel that might be viewed as her own fairy tale.

Figure 7.   Castle on the Hill
Gustave Doré's gothic castle suggests Château Saint-Louis in
Cather's Quebec.
(Illustration by Gustave Doré, from Perrault's Fairy Tales)

Shadows on the Rock: Willa Cather's Fairy Tale

Certainly Willa Cather's interest in fairy tale appears to have lasted a lifetime, or at least through her tenth novel. When she wrote *Shadows on the Rock,* Cather again composed a fairy tale, as conscious in form as "The Princess Baladina." To understand this intention is to see at last why Cather created so many effects in this novel that have bothered critics. The novel's flat characters and lack of dramatic tension, for example, contribute to the reader-pleasing atmosphere that from its first appearance made it one of Cather's best-selling novels. Readers have loved it without knowing exactly why. But looking at *Shadows* through the lens of fairy tale helps to understand its appeal: it strikes those same subconscious chords in us, satisfies us in the same primal way that fairy tales have done for so many generations. All human beings have a deep need for order, for the belief that good will prevail over evil, that by establishing a human bond it is possible to live happily ever after. These are some of the basic messages of fairy tale, and these, too, are the messages in *Shadows on the Rock.*

At the time she wrote *Shadows,* Cather planned to dedicate the book to the Menuhin children, to whom she was deeply attached at the time and continued to be for the rest of her life.[1] She refrained from doing so only because the talented children's mother disliked unnecessary publicity. Cather's initial impulse, however, recalls those stories full of enchantment which she wrote for her brothers when they were children, such as "The Strategy of Were-Wolf Dog" and "Jack-a-Boy,"[2] now part of that early work that Cather wished to bury.

Phyllis Robinson reminds us that Cather wrote *Shadows* just after the sudden death of her father and while her mother was dying of a stroke. In fact, Cather told her friend Dorothy Canfield Fisher that "the book had been her rock of refuge, the only thing in her life that held together and stayed the same" (Robinson 258). All Cather's biographers agree this period was a crisis point in her life; Robinson goes so far as to say she never fully recovered (255). One reasonably guesses that the experience of losing her parents might have caused

Willa Cather to seek refuge in a childhood world, one which she creates for herself in *Shadows*—an absolutely secure world, built upon a rock, protected from the savage forest by water, filled with protecting fathers and mothers, a place "where nothing changed . . . where the death of the King, the probable evils of a long regency, would never touch them" (280). Cather once again, as she does in *My Ántonia,* attempts to create a world where "[e]verything was as it should be" (*MA* 347).

Sharon O'Brien, in *Willa Cather: The Emerging Years,* argues that Cather's own search for the mother is threaded throughout her fiction. Isabelle McClung, Annie Fields, and Sarah Orne Jewett, according to O'Brien, all represented some aspect of the mother to Cather. All were lost—Isabelle by marriage to Jan Hambourg, and Fields and Jewett by death, recapitulating for Cather the infant sense of mother-loss. One can guess, if this is the case, the extreme anxiety Cather would feel when her natural mother's death was imminent. Cather escapes from this sense of loss and exclusion when her own mother is dying by writing *Shadows,* a novel of inclusion in every way.

Cather readers are aware of her near-obsession with childhood, for she returns to it again and again in her fiction and extols it in her nonfiction. Although she was fifty-eight when she published *Shadows,* Cather was facing in a real and major way, with the loss of both parents in such a short time, a basic human fear—"separation anxiety—the fear of being deserted" (*B* 15).[3] Some of her major characters exhibit this fear; Jim Burden overcomes it only when he is reunited at the end with Ántonia and becomes one of Cuzak's boys. Under the circumstances in which she lived at the time, I think Willa Cather deliberately decided to add a fairy-tale dimension to her historical novel about Quebec—for herself and for the children.[4] Furthermore, she gives her readers a specific clue to what she is about within the text of the novel. In the early pages of *Shadows on the Rock* Cather tells us that her heroine Cécile Auclair often read to her father the fables of La Fontaine (17). This direct reference within the text is just the kind of clue that Bernice Slote has admonished scholars for neglecting.

Jean de la Fontaine, a seventeenth-century French poet, wrote a series of fables in verse, most derived from classical sources such as Aesop. La Fontaine continues to be the best-known writer in France, a perpetual bestseller, and French children for generations have learned his fables by heart: "[T]hus most French people who have no other knowledge of literature have at least some acquaintance with La Fontaine" (Biard ix).[5] Willa Cather, an inveterate francophile and a lover of fairy tales besides, would undoubtedly have known La Fontaine well. Slote says that by "the spring of 1896 Willa Cather was familiar with most of the important French writers" (*KA* 365). Moreover, while Cather was editor of the *Home Monthly* in Pittsburgh, she went once or twice a week to the home of fellow-journalist George Seibel to read French literature in the original. In his article about Cather Seibel says of their reading nights, "It was the wildest rodeo of French literature ever put on between Paris, France, and Paris, Texas" (*SF* xix). La Fontaine's fables, France's best-loved reading, could hardly have been omitted from such a rodeo.

Cather's early newspaper and magazine articles prove her general knowledge of and taste for French literature; *The Kingdom of Art* and *The World and the Parish* contain a significant number of enthusiastic and complimentary pieces on French writers, books, and plays. French critic Michel Gervaud says that Cather was "deeply involved with the finest literature produced in our country" (*AWC* 72). He says, however, that her allusions to seventeenth-century French literature are rare, concluding that her primary interest was nineteenth-century French literature, and that she was less familiar with that of the seventeenth. Gervaud cites a reference to Molière in a 1902 Journal article and an allusion to Pascal in *Death Comes for the Archbishop*[6] as Cather's only references to seventeenth-century writers (72). He fails to note Cather's reference to Madame de Sévigné, a major seventeenth-century writer, on the same page of *Archbishop* in which she mentions Pascal. These two seventeenth-century writers, Pascal and Madame de Sévigné, were the Archbishop's favorites in his waning years. It is possible that in the author's waning years they were also her own.

Gervaud also fails to mention Cather's reference to La Fontaine in *Shadows on the Rock*. Interestingly, both protagonists in these sequential novels read not only great seventeenth-century French writers, but also writers who in a minor way interacted socially at the fringes of the court of King Louis XIV. This court defines the Old World which furnishes the backdrop for the drama in *Shadows*. Madame de Sévigné mentions Pascal and La Fontaine in her letters, which the Archbishop and his creator loved to read, and in them amusedly recounts to her daughter some of the fables. Some minor correspondence even exists between Madame de Sévigné and Pascal. It may be appropriate to mention also that Charles Perrault wrote his equally famous fairy tales, many of which were retold by the Grimm brothers in Germany in the next century, for the amusement of this same court.

Once Cather drops a name like La Fontaine's within her text, a creative Cather reader must then ask, "Why?" For one thing, fables like La Fontaine's, Perrault's fairy tales, and saints' and local legends delighted the culture about which Cather writes in *Shadows*—French Quebec just before the Age of Enlightenment. According to Swiss folklorist Max Lüthi, these tales were "for centuries one of the most vital and influential art forms in Europe" (*LO* 136). With the extensive and careful research Cather did for *Shadows,* she would quickly have spotted the role such tales played in the culture.

One of the predominant themes of Cather's fiction is the meaning and nature of art, and her own artistic credo that "the higher processes of art all lead toward simplification" indicates a receptivity to such simple art forms. It would be consistent with her thought to approach fables, fairy tales, and legends as works of art, and to incorporate them into her own art. Indeed, she had written her previous novel, *Death Comes for the Archbishop,* "something in the style of legend," and had drawn heavily upon saints' legends and local legends in the Santa Fé, New Mexico area for her material. Her reference to La Fontaine within the text may hint that her next novel is written "something in the style of fable." But scholars who have pursued Cather's textual references know that there is always more to unravel, that there is always something more specifically pertinent in one of her clues.

In the first place, the fables of La Fontaine are a series of tales, usually with a moral, in which animals are frequently personified. In *Shadows,* Cather strings a series of stories together, much as La Fontaine did with his fables, implies appropriate morals, and then describes characters by analogies to animals. The stories she includes in the novel combine features of fables, fairy tales, and saints' and local legends. Max Lüthi is very specific about the interrelationship and overlapping of these three types of stories. Furthermore, most of the stories within *Shadows,* in the tradition of fable, are told orally, almost always to Cécile, who is the repository of stories, another way in which she becomes the preserver and transmitter of civilization.[7] Those stories that are not conveyed orally are pondered upon in tale form by the characters, a technique Cather uses throughout the novel.[8] Many of these tales provide fable-like morals, miracles, and figures and motifs from fairy tale.

But the parallels are not only general but specific as well. One of the most arresting similarities between La Fontaine's fables and *Shadows* exists in their structures. La Fontaine's first volume of fables (1668) is divided into six books and an epilogue, exactly like Cather's novel. Critics have been puzzled by Cather's epilogue, since the novel might easily end with the last book; the epilogue appears to be an afterthought, yet we know Cather tried never to publish hastily constructed and unpolished fiction. Not coincidentally, when she wrote *Shadows* Cather seems to have appropriated La Fontaine's structure. Perhaps she needed an epilogue because she was submitting to a particular form.

Cather further develops her link to La Fontaine through her animal images and analogies. Thus, "La Grenouille," the frog, is the mother of little Jacques, making him "the frog's son" (58). In fairy tale the frog is a symbol of sexual fulfillment; since Cather's "La Grenouille," 'Toinette Gaux, is a prostitute, one might deduce that she had this association in mind. "L'Escargot," the snail, 'Toinette's only friend, "with her hair curled very tight and her hands hidden under her apron" (205), is the woman who lives with the frog. Cécile is called "little monkey" (173) by Pierre; Pierre is described as "quick as an otter" (170); and the baker is named "Pigeon." The hare-lipped butter-maker is called Madame Renaude-le-lièvre, or the rabbit, while the shoemaker Pommier "looked like a black bear standing upright" (78). Furthermore, Pommier in French means "apple tree," reminding us that personifying trees is one of the standard conventions of fairy tale, and that apple trees as well as apples figure significantly in many tales. A shoemaker, too, is a frequently appearing figure in fairy tale. Many classic fairy tales also include transmuted characters, "The Frog Prince" being one of the most commonly recognized types. Here little Jacques, the son of the frog, is also recognized by old Bishop Laval as "one of the least of these," thus a surrogate for Christ.

Other similarities exist between Cather's novel and La Fontaine's fables as well. La Fontaine's aim, "to stimulate the complex workings of poetic imagination in the reader and . . . to preserve clarity of thought and simplicity of expression in the actual text" (Biard 14) sounds startlingly like Cather's own credo. La Fontaine, like Cather, connected clarity and simplicity with grace and elegance, and concealed "technical perfection and ingeniousness under the veil of apparent ease and simplicity" (Biard 16). He, like Cather, preferred the suggestive to the exhaustive, and refused to overintellectualize language, to resort to abstractions: instead, he insisted upon using "le mot propre" (Biard 40). Both writers use archaism to achieve a poetic effect, to give their works "the quaint aspect and the charm of a seasoned antique" (Biard 165). Both Cather's *Shadows* and La Fontaine's fables create and comment upon patriarchal societies with rigid hierarchies, and societies which actually overlap. La Fontaine's fables satirize the court of Louis XIV, as Cather gently questions similar hierarchies supported by this court in Quebec. La Fontaine's lion represents the most important person—the king—and the mouse the least important, while in *Shadows* this same range of classes is represented by Count Frontenac and little Jacques.

Once we have begun to unravel *Shadows* with Cather's clue to La Fontaine and have established connections with the fables, we can then expand to fairy tale. In an article in *Religion and Literature,* Merrill M. Skaggs argues that Cather deliberately chose in *Shadows* to challenge the rules of fiction which insist that one cannot write a good novel about a good girl.[9] But of course a further extension of the argument is that one cannot write a novel and make a fairy tale. Yet that is another challenge Cather embraces here. And in fairy tales, if not in most gripping novels, the central character is *usually* a good girl. In fairy tale the princess, who is the most important person in her society, is as "authority-accepting, home-loving, law-abiding, credulous, generous and kind" (28) as Cécile Auclair, who conforms in every way to the prescription for a fairy-tale princess.

Like many other princesses, Cécile is motherless, but she has learned to keep house in perfect order for a protecting male, in this case her father. In fact, the spotless housekeeping of a dispossessed princess might be considered a fairy-tale motif, since it is found in so many tales. Snow White keeps as tidy a house for the dwarfs as does Cécile for her father, and the princess in "The Twelve Brothers," a Grimm brothers' classic, who "fetched the wood for cooking, and the vegetables, and watched the pots on the fire, so that supper was always ready when the others came in. She also kept great order in the house, and the beds were always beautifully white and clean" (Grimms 45). Housekeeping princesses, along with Cécile, take great pride in their linens and pots and brooms, which signify order and security and define for them a meaningful role. "These coppers, big and little, these brooms and clouts and brushes, were tools; and with them one made . . . life itself" (198).

A fairy-tale princess symbolizes beauty, goodness and perfection, and, like all fairy-tale characters, exists as a two-dimensional rather than a fully developed character. She is passive rather than active, and applauded for what she *is* rather than what she *does*. She is absolutely obedient to her father, who is often a weak man, and he in turn loves her most of all. When she is of age her hand is won in marriage, often by a soldier or an indigent adventurer, who proves in some way that he is the best man in the land. "The focus is always on the action of the fairy tale hero. . . . [H]andsomeness is only an accompanying characteristic" (*LF* 13). The fair is won by the fair, signifying that "the very best has been achieved, everything has turned out well" (*LF* 13). After marriage they rule the kingdom together—happily ever after, of course, proof that justice exists in the world and continuity is dependable. This most famous of fairy-tale formulae is Cécile Auclair's, the story which binds this string of Quebec stories together. Pierre Charron, a "soldier of fortune," is as handsome, proud, chivalrous, vain and brave (172) as any fairy-tale prince, and to Cécile his "daring and his pride seemed to her even more splendid than Count Frontenac's" (268).

The typical age for the hero or heroine of fairy tale is fifteen, the age when the Sleeping Beauty pricks her finger and Rapunzel's tears heal the eyes of her blinded prince. Fifteen was a magic age to Willa Cather; she says in a 1921 interview, "When I sit down to write, turns of phrase I've forgotten for years come back like white ink before fire. I think that most of the basic material a writer works with is acquired before he is fifteen" (*SF* xxvi). This age seems to signify for Cather the end of childhood; in fairy tale, fifteen is the time of transition from childhood to adulthood.[10] Nellie Birdseye is fifteen when she first meets Myra Henshawe, and Douglass in "The Treasure of Far Island" says to Margie when they set foot on the island where they played together as children, "Do you know, Margie, it makes me seem *fifteen* [my emphasis] again to feel this sand crunching under my feet" (*SF* 278).

When this story opens, Cécile Auclair is "a little girl of twelve, beginning to grow tall" (9). She celebrates her thirteenth birthday just before the ships return in July. After her river journey to visit the Harnois on the Ile d'Orleans with Pierre, where Cécile is confronted for the first time with the "real" world, in which beauty and ugliness, order and disorder exist together, she comes home feeling "as if she had grown at least two years older in the two nights she had been away" (197). Thus Cécile feels not thirteen but fifteen when the action ends. Further, Jeanne Le Ber, the character in *Shadows* who represents Cécile's exact opposite, is fifteen when she returns from school and begins to withdraw. Giorgio the drummer boy is fifteen when he leaves home to seek his fortune as a soldier in true fairy-tale style, and Count de Frontenac begins his military life at fifteen. Quite clearly, Cather's idea of a magic age consistent with fairy-tale thresholds permeates her chronologies.

Jeanne Le Ber's story is as replete with fairy-tale conventions as Cécile's, and is juxtaposed against Cécile's as a kind of anti–fairy tale. Jeanne le Ber is the only daughter of the richest man in Montreal, and true to fairy-tale convention, he loves her the most, more than any of his five sons. Jacques Le Ber adopts the orphaned Pierre Charron and raises him like a son, expecting him to marry his daughter and perpetuate his legacy. Interestingly, if Pierre is counted as one of Jeanne's brothers, she then has six. The story of a single princess with six brothers, such as Grimms' "The Six Swans," is familiar in the fairy-tale canon.

Instead, Jeanne Le Ber imprisons herself in her room at fifteen, refusing to accept the jewels and gowns her father wants to give her as befits a coming-of-age princess, or to take the perfect husband he has provided for her. Jeanne Le Ber plays out the Sleeping Beauty motif, complete with a magic spinning wheel which is miraculously repaired while she is cloistered in her cell in the church, a story the villagers accept as if she has sent them "a blooming rosetree" (130). In the Grimms' story, the Sleeping Beauty's name is Briar Rose. Further, before a prince can rescue her, the hedge of thorns surrounding her castle must bloom into roses.

Unlike the Sleeping Beauty, Jeanne Le Ber refuses to wake up and accept the responsibilities of adulthood, to come to love her duties (24) like Cécile, and to provide civilization with continuity. One of the primary responsibilities of a princess is to make her father happy, but Jeanne Le Ber's father "was never the same man after she shut herself away" (178), and his house became "the tomb of his hopes" (133). Her own face, once rosy, "fresh and soft, like . . . apple blossoms" (179) became "like a stone face" (182); turning a character to stone is one of the conventional punishments for evil in fairy tales. And, too, her voice became crowlike, a reminder of numerous tales in folklore in which characters are changed into birds, such as Grimms' "The Seven Ravens." Also within the Jeanne Le Ber story is the motif of Pierre's three rescues from death by the magic intervention of his betrothed.

Folklorists tell us that fairy tale portrays an imperishable, eternal world that triumphs over time and the passage of time, just the kind of world Cather creates in *Shadows*. Fairy tale uses a variety of techniques for creating this sense of timelessness and imperishability. Everything in the world of fairy tale is

clearly and neatly fashioned, "simple . . . but definite" (64);[11] objects and people are sharply outlined, but they exist only in outline. Characters' inner feelings
are never portrayed in any depth. There is a predilection for everything clearly
formed, in colors as well as in shape, and for objects which give the sense of
definiteness, firmness, clarity—cities, castles, rooms, boxes, jewels, swords.
Shadows is one of Cather's most detailed novels, and the reader comes away
with just such clear and definite images: the Gothic rock-set city, surrounded
by water like a castle moat and crowned by a palace; the Auclairs' living room,
with its red sofa and table set before the fire with crystal and silver; Giorgio the
little drummer boy in front of the Chateau's gates, in his "blue coat, high boots,
and a three-cornered hat" (55); the Canadian sky that shines "with a blue to
ravish the heart" (104).

Fairy tale makes use of "everything metallic and mineral, for gold and
silver, . . . glass and crystal" (*LO* 45) to create this sense of definiteness and
imperishability. These elements also represent and express the highest degree
of beauty. Glass mountains, slippers, and coffins come to mind along with
golden hair and silver hands, golden apples and silver cups. Cather's rock on
which the action takes place is a symbol of such permanence, as is the Count's
crystal bowl full of glass fruit, one of the primary symbols in the novel. Cather's
novel provides many such images: "the steeples were framed and encrusted with
gold" (228); "many kinds of gold, all gleaming in the soft, hyacinth-coloured
haze of autumn: wan sickly gold of the willows . . . bright gold of the birches,
copper gold of the beeches . . . tarnished gold of the elms" (229). Quebec stands
"gleaming above the river like an altar with many candles, or like a holy city
in an old legend, shriven, sinless, washed in gold" (169).

One of the chief characteristics of fairy tale is the use of absolutes and
oppositions, extremes and contrasts, all favorite Cather devices. *Shadows,* more
than any of her other novels, is based upon absolutes in opposition, and ambi-
guities are rare. Good daughters are juxtaposed against bad daughters; good
mothers against bad mothers; good fathers, sons, and protectors against bad.
The security and safety of the rock on which Quebec is built is juxtaposed
against the insecurity and hostility of the forest, a fairy-tale forest, indeed, a
"black pine forest" which "came down to the water's edge" and "stretched no
living man knew how far" (6). Jacques le Ber is the richest man in the community, while little Jacques is the poorest boy. Bichet the tortured is juxtaposed
against Blinker the torturer. Chabanel the martyr-priest retches on Indian dog
meat, while Pierre Charron finds it tasty enough cooked with blueberries.

Shadows abounds with fairy-tale characters and images: a king (Louis IV);
a count (Frontenac); a magician (Auclair, who is an apothecary); Cécile the
good princess, and Jeanne le Ber the bad princess; good mothers like Cécile's
and the Church mothers, and bad mothers like 'Toinette Gaux and Countess
Frontenac; good fathers like Auclair, and bad fathers like Blinker's, who taught

him a torturer's trade. We have an "old woman with a crutch" (79), the crone
of fairy tale; the giant in the Count's dream, "a very tall man in a plumed hat
and huge boots—a giant, in fact; the little boy's head did not come up to his
boot-tops" (244); and Blinker, a kind of ogre who sleeps either in a cave or in
the ashes by the stove and is "so ill-favoured that nobody wanted him about"
(15). When the Count dies, his heart is sealed in a casket, fairy-tale style. Old
Bishop Laval wears a pair of slippers which might well belong to one of the
twelve dancing princesses: "a beautiful pair of red satin slippers, embroidered
in gold and purple, with leather soles and red leather heels" (81).

Max Lüthi says that "fairy tale is a universe in miniature" (*LO* 24), as well
as an exaggeratedly artificial one. Cather uses the words "little" and "artificial"
innumerable times in this novel. Quebec is "the little capital" (4) which looks
like "one of those little artificial mountains which were made in the churches at
home to present a theatric scene of the Nativity" (5). Indeed, the sense of scale
in *Shadows* is miniature, diminutive, exactly opposite from Cather's previous
novel *Archbishop* where the sense of vastness and space is part of its power.
Phyllis Rose calls Cather a writer with a "sense of scale" (137), and nowhere is
this concept more apparent than in contrasting the opposite scales of these two
sequential novels together.

Cather herself reminds us throughout that this world is an artificial one,
"not a tangled, disorderly waxing and waning nature . . . but a shaped, limited,
unchanging one" (*LF* 18). The artifice of this world is symbolized by the
Count's glass fruit, which Cécile treasures and finds so much lovelier than real
fruit. When the Count dies, he gives the fruit to Cécile, who then becomes its
custodian. Perhaps Cather is suggesting here that Cécile and her world are as
unreal as the glass fruit—most beautiful when held up to the light, but hollow.[12]
Furthermore, Saint Cecelia is known as the patron saint of the blind, as well as
of music. Cather may be implying that Cécile is blind to the world of reality.

In an early newspaper article Cather writes, "Surely we all know that the
books we read when we were children shaped our lives; at least they shaped our
imaginings, and it is with our imaginings that we live" (*WP* 852). According to
Bruno Bettelheim, childhood readers of fairy tales retain the images forever,
and reading them becomes "a frame of reference for comprehending the world"
(45). Willa Cather's fiction bears enough evidence to prove that fairy tales were
a part of her psychological makeup, both consciously and unconsciously. If, as
Lüthi says, fairy tales "remove us from the time continuum and make us feel
that there is another way of viewing and experiencing life, that behind all birth
and death there is another world, resplendent, imperishable and incorruptible"
(*LO* 45), perhaps Willa Cather did turn to an old and familiar and safe place for
comfort. The real miracle of this novel may be having such a place to return to
in troubled times. Cather's own childhood images become the "crag where . . .
human beings built themselves nests in the rock, and held fast" (226).

In another early article Cather writes of *Alice in Wonderland*, "If I knew of any country as fair and genial as that Wonderland I visited so long ago, I would go there and take up my abode forever" (*WP* 360). In *Shadows on the Rock* she creates herself such a Wonderland, a temporary haven at best. Looking at this novel as Cather's Wonderland, however, alters our critical interpretation and appreciation.

A line from *Through the Looking-Glass* reads, "Thy loving smile will surely hail / The love-gift of a fairy-tale." According to Bettelheim, "To decide whether a story is a fairy tale or something entirely different one might ask whether it could rightly be called a love-gift to a child" (27). Using this definition, Willa Cather's *Shadows on the Rock* clearly qualifies. In this intended love gift to three children, Cather's struggle to love her life, "mean as it is" when she writes, becomes a struggle to love herself, to love life itself. In risking that struggle, in the prize it gained her, Willa Cather seems triumphant.

Appendix

Cather's References to Fairy Tales, Folk Tales, and Legends (Arranged Chronologically)

The Troll Garden

On the title page is a quotation from Charles Kingsley's *The Roman and the Teuton:* "A fairy palace, with a fairy garden; . . . inside the trolls dwell, . . . working at their magic forges, making and making always things rare and strange."

"Flavia and Her Artists"

1. "Perhaps it was a vague curiosity to see Flavia's husband, who had been the magician of her childhood and the hero of innumerable Arabian fairy tales" (149).

2. "Flavia, had, indeed, quite an equipment of epigrams to the effect that our century creates the iron genii which evolve its fairy tales . . . " (152).

3. " . . . Imogen, beginning to feel very much like Alice in Wonderland . . ." (154).

4. "There was about the darkened room some suggestion of certain chambers in the Arabian Nights . . . " (155).

5. " . . . he pulled her up the river to hunt for fairy knolls . . . " (160).

6. "Her own inclination had been for serious stories, with sad endings, like the Little Mermaid. . . . Then she found the story of the Little Mermaid herself, and forgot him" (161).

7. "And you, Miss Willard, did you dream of the White Rabbit or the little mermaid?" (162).

8.   " . . . he is not in the fairy story in that he sees these people exactly as they are, *but* he is utterly unable to see Flavia as they see her" (164).

9.   " . . . you must needs get the Little Mermaid's troubles to grieve over" (167).

10.   "She was reminded of the fury of the crowd in the fairy tale, when once the child called out that the king was in his night clothes" (168).

11.   "Just wait until Flavia's black swans have flown!" (171).

"The Sculptor's Funeral"

1.   "Whatever he touched, he revealed its holiest secret; liberated it from enchantment and restored it to its pristine loveliness, like the Arabian prince who fought the enchantress spell for spell" (180).

"The Garden Lodge"

1.   "The garden to the left and the orchard to the right had never been so riotous with spring, and had burst into impassioned bloom, as if to accommodate Caroline, though she was certainly the last woman to whom the witchery of Freya could be attributed" (187).

2.   " . . . she thought of the Arabian fairy tale in which the Genii brought the princess of China to the sleeping prince of Damascus, and carried her through the air back to her palace at dawn" (196).

"A Death in the Desert"

1.   Central to this story is the motif of two brothers, which Cather uses in many of her fictions.

2.   Everett "remembered going through a looking-glass labyrinth when he was a boy, and trying gallery after gallery, only at every turn to bump his nose against his own face—which, indeed, was not his own, but his brother's" (210).

Alexander's Bridge

1.   "She's [Hilda Burgoyne] really Mac Connell's poetic motif, you see; makes the whole thing a fairy tale" (24).

2.   "When she [Hilda] began to dance, by way of showing the gossoons what she had seen on the fairy rings at night, the houses broke into a prolonged uproar" (25).

O, Pioneers!

1.   "I'm going to paint some slides for it on glass, out of the *Hans Andersen* [my italics] book" (17).

2.   Ivar's resemblances to the troll of Scandinavian folklore are unmistakable. He lives in an underground dwelling, and is described as follows: "He was a queerly shaped old man, with a thick powerful body set on short bowlegs. His shaggy white hair, falling in a thick mane about his ruddy cheeks, made him look older than he was. He was barefoot . . . " (37).

3.   "She knew long portions of the 'Frithjof Saga' by heart, and . . . was fond of Longfellow's verse,—the ballads and the 'Golden Legend' and 'The Spanish Student' " (61).

4.   "Things away from home often look better than they are. You know what your *Hans Andersen* [my italics] book says . . . " (62).

The Song of the Lark

1.   " . . . her delicate, tender chin—the one soft touch in her hard little Scandinavian face, as if some fairy godmother had caressed her there and left a cryptic promise" (10).

2.   "And it was Summer, beautiful Summer! Those were the closing words of Thea's favorite fairy tale . . . " (22).

3.   Thirty-year-old Ray Kennedy planned to marry twelve-year-old Thea when she was old enough, and "keep her like a queen" (53). His last words to her are, "She's a queen!" (149).

4.   Wuensch tells Thea that some people "have nothing inside them. . . . They are like the ones in the 'Märchen,' a grinning face and hollow in the insides" (78). This quotation reaffirms Cather's awareness of these tales and their characteristics.

5.   "Shipwrecks come and go, *Märchen* come and go, but the river keeps right on" (190).

6.   "I didn't know I had it in me, Thea. I thought it was all a fairy tale" (360).

7.   " . . . among other legendary things the legendary theme of the absolutely magical power of a beautiful woman" (372).

8.   "I always halfway believe the fairy tales he spins me" (387).

9.   "It isn't polite to mention what he is, outside of the Arabian Nights" (388).

10.   "This woman he had never known; she had somehow devoured his little friend, as the wolf ate up Red Ridinghood" (412).

11.   " . . . we don't get fairy tales in this world . . . " (468).

12.   "She had always insisted, against all evidence, that life was full of fairy tales, and it was!" (489).

My Ántonia

1.   " . . . the yellow leaves and shining white bark made them look like the gold and silver trees in *fairy tales* [my italics]" (62).

2.   Incorporated within this novel is the folktale, probably German in origin, of two men in a sleigh who feed people one at a time to a pack of wolves pursuing the sleigh (56).

3.   "Our tree became the talking tree of the *fairy tale* [my italics]; legends and stories nestled like birds in its branches" (83).

4.   Some fairy-tale figures and images in *Ántonia:*

   a.   " . . . there was an old beggar woman who went about selling herbs and roots she had dug up in the forest" (39).

   b.   Pavel and Peter fit the Grimms' tale type number 60—"The Two Brothers" (see *LF* 99).

   c.   Loving grandfather and grandmother who live in a storybook house.

   d.   Mushrooms gathered in a "deep Bohemian forest" (79). (See p. 27 for more complete list.)

5.   Jim says that he "used to think with pride that Ántonia, like Snow-White in the fairy tale, was still the fairest of them all" (215).

One of Ours

1.   Claude Wheeler is an example of the hero who "appears as a dumbell or . . . a Cinderella, as underestimated, despised, or disadvantaged" (*LO* 130). Certainly the hero journey can be made to apply to this novel.

2.   "Her hazel eyes peered expectantly over her nose-glasses, always watching to see things turn out wonderfully well; always looking for some good German fairy on the cupboard or the cake-box—or in the steaming vapor of wash day" (41).

3. " . . . another gold day stretched before him like a glittering carpet . . . " (78).

4. " . . . in a flash he would be transformed from a wooden post into a real boy" (103).

The Professor's House

1. "If he had taken this, it might have been like the wooden cups that were always revealing *Amis* and *Amile* to each other" (131).

2. "I was thinking . . . about Euripides; how, when he was an old man, he went and lived by the sea, and it was thought queer at the time. It seems that houses had become insupportable to him" (156).

3. "We had *Robinson Crusoe* with us, and Roddy's favourite book, *Gulliver's Travels,* which he never tired of" (188).

4. "I got the better of the Spanish grammar and read the twelve books of the *Aeneid*" (251).

5. "When I look into the *Aeneid* now, I can always see two pictures: the one on the page, and another behind that" (252).

6. "He remembered some lines from a translation from the Norse he used to read long ago . . . : 'For thee a house was built / Ere thou wast born: / For thee a mould was made / Ere thou of woman came'" (272).

My Mortal Enemy

1. "I thought of the place as being under a spell, like Sleeping Beauty's palace; it had been in a trance, or lain in its flowers like a beautiful corpse . . . " (17). The assumption is that the phrase "lain in its flowers like a beautiful corpse" refers to Snow White.

2. " . . . a fur hat on her head, with a single narrow garnet feather sticking out behind, like the pages' caps in old story books" (20).

Death Comes for the Archbishop

1. A primary archetypal pattern is the fairy-tale motif of the two brothers.

2. Many of Cather's characters in this novel are legendary: Archbishop Lamy, Father Machebeuf, and Kit Carson, for example.

3. Cather incorporates saints' and local legends into her narrative:

    a.   Juan Diego and the legend of Our Lady of Guadalupe (46).

    b.   Legend of Fray Baltazar at Ácoma (103).

    c.   Martinez and Lucero (139).

    d.   Legend of Father Junípero Serra (279).

4.   Cather touches on the Indian legends of the ceremonial fire in a cave which sapped the strength of the young men, as well as on legends of snake worship.

5.   The tale of the murdering innkeeper, which Cather uses in "The Lonely Road to Mora," is a major fairy-tale motif.

6.   " . . . Virgin-daughter, Virgin-mother, girl of the people and Queen of Heaven: *le rêve suprême de la chair*. The nursery tale could not vie with Her in simplicity, the wisest theologians could not match Her in profundity" (256).

Shadows on the Rock

1.   " . . . he and his daughter usually spent the long evening very happily without visitors. She read aloud to him, the fables of La Fontaine . . . " (17).

2.   Saints' and local legends are incorporated into this novel:

    a.   Catherine de Saint-Augustin (40).

    b.   Saint Edmond, Archbishop of Cantorbéry (85).

    c.   Jeanne Le Ber (130).

    d.   Stories of Father Hector (139) and Father Chabanel (150).

Obscure Destinies

"Old Mrs. Harris"

1.   "She had stopped at a very German picture of Gretchen entering the church, with Faustus gazing at her from behind a rose tree, Mephisto at his shoulder" (106).

2.   "Vickie began: 'Day of wrath, upon that day / The world to ashes melts away, / As David and the Sibyl say'" (107).

3.   "Mr. Templeton told *Uncle Remus* stories . . . " (162).

4.   " . . . she was repeating a passage from the second part of *Pilgrim's Progress* . . . (183).*

Lucy Gayheart

1.   Lucy is another of Cather's "princesses," a "watchmaker's daughter" (21), "poor as a church mouse" (22), who searches for her identity through males, and destroys herself because of "romance."

2.   One of the characters is called "Fairy Blair."

The Old Beauty and Others

"The Best Years"

1.   " . . . it was a hall, in the old baronial sense, reminded her of the lines in their *Grimm's Fairy Tales* book: 'Return, return thou youthful bride, / This is a robbers' hall inside' " (111).

Uncle Valentine and Other Stories

"Uncle Valentine"

1.   "I've got a new collection of all the legends about Tristan and Iseult" (19).

2.   "He . . . commenced to play the Ballad of the Young Knight, which begins: 'From the Ancient Kingdoms, / Through the wood of dreaming . . . ' " (19).

3.   "We knew it was the moon, but we could see no form, no solid image. . . . 'The Rhinegold!' . . . " (25).

"Double Birthday"

1.   " . . . he resembled a satyr . . . " (46).

2.   "Perhaps he dreamed of that unfortunate young singer whom he sometimes called . . . 'the lost Lenore' " (47).

3.   "That winter and spring he lived like a man lost in a dark morass, the Slave in the Dismal Swamp. He suffered more than his Gretchen . . . " (52).

4.   "If Mephistopheles were to emerge from the rhododendrons and stand behind his shoulder with such an offer, he wouldn't hesitate" (55).

"Ardessa"

1.   "Ardessa's employer, like young Lochinvar, had come out of the West . . ." (101).

2.   "Like a Sultan's bride, she was inviolate in her lord's absence . . . " (103).

"Coming, Eden Bower"

1.   "The priest . . . taught him to like *Don Quixote* and *The Golden Legend . . .*" (146).

2.   "The spot seemed enchanted; as if a vision out of Alexandria, out of the remote pagan past, had bathed itself there in Helianthine fire" (151).

3.   " . . . she had no geographical associations; unless with Crete, or Alexandria, or Veronese's Venice. She was the immortal perception, the perennial theme" (153).

4.   The Aztec legend, "The Forty Lovers of the Queen," is incorporated into this story, a technique Cather uses again elsewhere. This is a legend about a princess/queen.

5.   "Tomorrow night the wind would blow again, and this mask would be the golden face of Clytemnestra"(176).

Willa Cather's Collected Short Fiction

"On the Gull's Road"

1.   Alexandra Ebbing is another of Cather's "princesses," with "her white throat and arms and red-gold hair" . . . (80). Her beautiful face is "proud and sad and tender, and strangely calm. The curve of the lips could not have been cut more clearly with the most delicate instrument, and whatever shade of feeling passed over them seemed to partake of their exquisiteness" (80).

2.   " . . . lights began to glow like luminous pearls along the water-front—the necklace of an irreclaimable queen" (83).

3.   "The sea before us was so rich and heavy and opaque that it might have been lapis lazuli. It was the blue of legend, simply; the color that satisfies like sleep" (85).

4.   "This is first cousin to the Pole waters, and the sea we have left is only a kind of fairy tale" (89).

"Eleanor's House"

1.   " . . . her preposterous skirts trailing behind her like the brier-torn gown of some wandering Griselda" (104).

"The Treasure of Far Island"

1.   "But you have done it as they used to do it in the fairy tales, without soiling your golden armor . . . " (273).

2.   "What plays have you been playing? Pirate or enchanted princess or Sleeping Beauty or Helen of Troy, to the disaster of men? Margie sighed as she awoke out of the fairyland" (273).

3.   "Oh, I wish I had some of the cake that Alice ate in Wonderland and could make you a little girl again" (275).

4.   " . . . the cow bells sounded faintly from the meadows along the shore like the bells of fairy cities ringing on the day the prince brought home his bride" (276).

5.   " . . . of all the possessions of their childhood's Wonderland, Far Island had been dearest. . . . They had even decided that a race of kindly dwarfs must inhabit it . . . " (276).

6.   "Then weep, my princess, for I will wake you now!" (281).

7.   "In the western sky the palaces of crystal and gold were quenched in night. . . . [O]ut of the east rose the same moon that has glorified all the romances of the world . . . " (282).

"Jack-a-Boy"

1.   " . . . Jack-a-Boy scudding down the pavement like a gleeful young elf, with the Professor in the role of a decrepit Old Man of the Mountain shuffling after him" (317).

2.   " . . . this was not a human child, but one of the immortal children of Greek fable made flesh for a little while" (318).

3.   "I want to know . . . about the white horses of Rhesus; I have forgotten who stole them" (319).

4.   " . . . the man of learning told that old, old story of Achilles' wrath" (319).

5.   "Perhaps some wood nymph, tall and fair, came in and laid her cool fingers on his brow and bore him off with the happy children of Pan" (320).

6.   "He rose from them, beautiful and still a child, like Cupid out of Psyche's arms" (320).

7.   "Why should he have liked the story of Theseus' boyhood in the Centaur's cave better than Jack the Giant Killer?" (320).

8.   "Why should he tell me that the two stars that peeped down into his crib between the white curtains were like the eyes of Golden Helen?" (321).

9.   "In my Homer over there there is a little, sticky thumbmark on the margin of the picture of the parting of Hector and Andromache" (321).

10.   " . . . the moon was . . . curved like Artemis' bow" (322).

"The Conversion of Sum Loo"

1.   "For once a god loved a maiden of Soutcheofou and gave her the charms of heaven and since then the women of that city have been the most beautiful in the Middle Kingdom and have lived but to love and be loved" (325). (Note: This quotation is repeated in "A Son of the Celestial.")

"A Singer's Romance"

1.   "Above her own face in the glass she saw the reflection of her maid's. Pretty, slender 'Toinette, with her satin-smooth skin and rosy cheeks . . . " (335). The use of the mirror motif here again signals that the older woman will be replaced by the younger one.

"Eric Hermannson's Soul"

1.   " . . . a girl, his sister . . . had been very near to his life ever since the days when they read fairy tales together and dreamed the dreams that never come true" (363).

2.   "He looks like a dragon-slayer" (365).

3.   " . . . if there are many such young Valkyries as Eric's sister among them, they would simply tie you up in a knot if they suspected you were guying them" (367).

4.   "Eric was . . . handsome as young Siegfried, a giant in stature, with a skin singularly pure and delicate, like a Swede's; hair as yellow as the locks of Tennyson's amorous Prince . . . " (368).

5.   " . . . he felt as the Goths before the white marbles in the Roman Capitol, not knowing whether they were men or gods" (370).

6. "The Puvis de Chavannes is even more beautiful than I thought it in Paris. A pale dream-maiden sits by a pale dream-cow . . . " (373).

7. "That arm could have thrown Thor's hammer . . . " (377).

"The Prodigies"

1. "The children would not stay in the nursery and poor Elsie has lost her 'Alice in Wonderland' and wails without ceasing because nurse cannot repeat 'The Walrus and the Carpenter' off hand" (411).

2. "We have read the legends of the Holy Grail and Frau Cosima Wagner gave us a book of the legends of the Nibelung Trilogy" (419).

"The Strategy of the Were-Wolf Dog"

This tale, published in *Home Monthly* in 1896, is Cather's attempt to write a legend, and contains all the characteristics of legend.

"A Night in the Greenaway Court"

1. "He had been there then for three months, dwelling in shameful idleness, one of that band of renegades who continually ate at my lord's table and hunted with his dogs and devoured his substance, waiting for some turn of fortune, like the suitors in the halls of Penelope" (485).

"The Clemency of the Court"

1. "The love of the plains was strong in him. It had always been so, ever since he was a little fellow, when the brown grass was up to his shoulders and the straw stacks were the golden mountains of fairyland" (520).

"A Son of the Celestial"

1. "For once a god had loved a woman of that city, and he gave her the charms of heaven, and since then the maidens of Soutcheofou have been the most beautiful in the Middle Kingdom, and have lived but to love and be loved" (525).

"A Tale of the White Pyramid"

1. "Memphis stood as silent as the judgment hall of Osiris" (529).

"The Princess Baladina—Her Adventure"

This story is Cather's own playful fairy tale; it contains all the characteristic ingredients: a princess with golden hair who plays with three golden balls; a king; a prince; a fairy godmother; a wizard; a miller's son.

Abbreviations

AB   Willa Cather. *Alexander's Bridge*. New York: A. A. Knopf, 1912.

Art   Bernice Slote and Virginia Faulkner, eds. *The Art of Willa Cather*. Lincoln: Univ. Nebraska Press, 1974.

AT   Willa Cather. *April Twilights*. Lincoln: Univ. of Nebraska Press, 1962.

B   Bruno Bettelheim. *The Uses of Enchantment*. New York: A. A. Knopf, 1975.

GL   Jacobus de Voragine. *The Golden Legend*. New York: Longmans, Green and Co., 1941.

KA   Willa Cather. *The Kingdom of Art*. Lincoln: Univ. of Nebraska Press, 1966.

LF   Max Lüthi. *The Fairytale as Art Form and Portrait of Man*. Bloomington: Indiana Univ. Press, 1984.

LO   _____ . *Once Upon A Time: On the Nature of Fairy Tales*. Bloomington: Indiana Univ. Press, 1984.

OW   Willa Cather. *On Writing*. New York: A. A. Knopf, 1949.

SF   _____ . *Willa Cather's Collected Short Fiction, 1892–1912*. Lincoln: Univ. of Nebraska Press, 1965.

W   Barbara G. Walker. *The Woman's Encyclopedia of Myths and Secrets*. San Francisco: Harper & Row, 1983.

WP   Willa Cather. *The World and the Parish*. Lincoln: Univ. of Nebraska Press, 1970.

Z   Jack Zipes. *Fairy Tales and the Art of Subversion*. London: Heinemann Educational Books, 1983.

Notes

Introduction

1. In *Willa Cather: The Emerging Years,* Sharon O'Brien attributes Cather's secrecy to her lesbianism. She says,

   "Cather's need to imply the presence of the 'not named' [her lesbianism] may also have contributed to her fiction the allusive, suggestive qualities we associate with modernism. The aesthetic of indirection she espoused in 'The Novel Demeuble' evokes at once the lesbian writer forced to conceal and the twentieth-century writer aware both of the inadequacies and the possibilities of language. . . . [B]ecause Cather could not tell the truth directly she was, at times, forced to tell it slant, and the resulting creative tension between expression and suppression produced novels that are subtle, richly symbolic, and ambiguous, enriched by the repressed, the hidden, and the covert. Ultimately her need both to disclose and to conceal lesbianism—one of the conflicts that threatened to silence the beginning writer—contributed to the pleasure she found in the creative process." (218)

2. John J. Murphy's *Critical Essays on Willa Cather* (Boston: G. K. Hall, 1984) contains several articles on Cather's references and allusions.

3. Specific references in the text of *O Pioneers!* are to Hans Christian Andersen. This fact is especially interesting since Andersen's fairy-tale heroes, like the characters in Cather's prairie novels, are often farmers, and his imagery is often derived from the farmyard. See the Appendix for specific allusions to Andersen's fairy tales.

4. Folklorists designate this genre in slightly different ways. "Folk-fairy" is a common term, and seems applicable to my topic. The hyphen here and in "fairy-tale" is optional. "Fairy-tale" is usually hyphenated when used as an adjective.

5. Cather's use of fairy tale is often alluded to by critics, although none to date have explored it. O'Brien refers to Cather's "The Profile" as a "fairy tale requiring psychological as well as literary exegesis" (49). She says that in Cather's "fairy tale" (49), Dunlap sees "himself as a fairy-tale prince" (49). She refers to Virginia as the "evil enchantress" (50) who is in love with her own reflection in a mirror. O'Brien concludes: "As the fairy-tale plot demonstrates, only a prince can hope to rescue and possess a princess" (50). O'Brien also states: " 'The Burglar's Christmas' is a dreamlike fairy tale of wish-fulfillment, not a consciously shaped narrative" (50).

6. "Mother and Daughter Share a Fulbright Year," *New York Times,* 14 Oct. 1986, I, 27:1.

7. Adeline Tintner addresses fairy tales in the work of Henry James in *The Pop World of Henry James,* published by UMI Research Press (1989).

8. We should note, however, that Hilda, the character connected to fairy tale, is Bartley Alexander's romantic illusion.

Chapter 1

1. Cather critics agree that *Lark* is a highly autobiographical novel. With this fact in mind, we may infer that with Thea's specialness Cather is indulging in a common childhood fantasy. Maria Tatar says:

    "A growing sense of dissatisfaction with his parents, stemming from a sense of being slighted or neglected, leads the child to seek relief in the idea that he must be a stepchild or an adopted child. Even after puberty, the child's imagination may be preoccupied with the task of ridding himself of his own parents and replacing them with those of higher social rank. He fancies himself the child of a prominent statesman, a millionaire, an aristocratic landowner—a person appointed with the very qualities in which his own parents seem most wanting. Such daydreams, Freud points out, serve as the 'fulfillment of wishes' and as a 'correction of actual life.'" (74)

2. According to Tatar: "The symbolic codes woven into fairy tales are relatively easy to decipher, for they are often based on familiar allusions or on readily decodable verbal substitutions. As Freud observed, folklore in general takes advantage of symbols that have universal validity. Kings and queens as a rule represent parents; a prince or princess signifies the self. A deep, impenetrable forest symbolizes the dark, hidden depths of the soul. A body of water is often associated with the process of birth" (80). All these noted symbols are present in *Lark*.

3. According to Stith Thompsons's folk tale classification, the major story line, or "type," of *Lark* is the hero journey, fairy tale's most common plot for a tale in which the protagonist is usually *male* instead of female. Here once again Cather reverses a fairy-tale situation. Thea's helpers on this journey are her fathers/princes: Dr. Archie, Ray Kennedy, Wuench, and Fred Ottenburg; each provides her with some ingredient essential to her journey.

4. Undertones of "Goldilocks" pervade this scene in which Thea's mother brings her breakfast on the morning she returns from Chicago. Her mother says, "I'll have to get you a longer bed. . . . You're getting too long for that one" (224).

5. Interestingly, Maria Tatar notes the dominating influence of fairy tale on Richard Wagner, especially in the *Ring* Cycle. Giannone informs us that Cather admits to having attempted to create the effect of a Wagnerian opera in *The Song of the Lark*.

6. Bettelheim says that fifteen was once the age when menstruation began. Fifteen is also Willa Cather's favorite age for a character to cross the threshold into adulthood. See page 62 for further discussion of Cather's fifteen-year-olds.

7. In *The Scarlet Letter,* Pearl's first tears symbolize her entry into the human community. Hawthorne was another of Cather's major literary mentors, as several scholars have noted.

8. The princess who wears out her shoes is a fairy-tale motif classified in Stith Thompson's index.

9. Like *Lark, Anna Karenina* involves an adulterous relationship. Anna eventually commits suicide as the result of her involvement with Vronsky, while Thea uses her affair with Fred as a necessary part of her own growth. Cather was criticized when *Lark* was published for her treatment of Thea's relationship with Fred.

10. Opals are the goddess's stone. Thus, the brothers are dressed appropriately to serve as acolytes.

11. Myra Henshawe is holding a guitar when she first meets Nellie Birdseye. Interpreting the guitar as a womb symbol adds meaning in both novels.

12. Thea's entrance into Panther Canyon is comparable to Jim Burden's arrival at the prairie, which can also be interpreted as his symbolic fairy-tale forest. Cather tells us the following about Thea: "The old fretted lines which marked one off, which defined her . . . were all *erased* [my italics]" (296). And then: "The high, sparkling air drank it [her old self] up like *blotting* paper [my italics]" (296). Similarly, Jim feels "erased, blotted out" (8) when he first arrives on the Nebraska prairie and begins forging a new identity. Cather uses similar wording in similar incidences in two subsequent fairy-tale-laden novels.

    See page 20 for further information on the fairy-tale forest. It should also be noted that there is no equivalent to the forest in the most common versions of "Cinderella."

13. The Sleeping Beauty's sleep symbolizes the long period of quiet concentration on oneself necessary in the process of making a transition between adolescence and adulthood. This sleep is ended by the prince's kiss (B 225).

14. Susan Rosowski likens the stream to a lover: "When she enters the pool, the stream seems a lover, a 'glittering thread of current [that] had a kind of lightly worn, loosely knit personality, graceful and laughing' (378)" (Rosowski 71). She suggests that Thea has consummated her love with the stream when Fred arrives, and that he is merely "a human correlative of the stream's maleness" (Rosowski 72).

15. Bettelheim discusses slipper as vagina in some detail in *The Uses of Enchantment*.

16. This brother/sister fairy-tale motif plays a significant part in the next novel, *My Ántonia;* Jim Burden finds wholeness when he is reunited with Antonia in a final image suggesting two siblings in the womb, "bedded down in the straw, wondering children, being taken we knew not whither" (*MA* 371). Sharon O'Brien discusses Cather's use of the brother/sister motif in *Willa Cather: The Emerging Voice*.

17. See pages 18 and 38 for further discussion of the mirror motif.

Chapter 2

1. Briggs illustrates this classification as follows: "Cinderella, for instance, is Type 510 and is composed of motifs S31: Cruel stepmother; L55: Stepdaughter heroine; F311.1: Fairy godmother; D1050.1: Clothes produced by magic; F861.4.3: Carriage from pumpkin; N711.6: Prince sees heroine at ball and is enamoured; C761.3: Taboo: staying too long at ball; must leave before certain hour; and H36.1: Slipper test" (*Fairies* xii).

    "Motif" is a difficult word to pin down in a specific definition. Thompson admits that "when the term 'motif' is employed, it is always in a very loose sense, and is made to include any of the elements of narrative structure" (19). He says, "I have tried to include all that becomes a part of tradition—all that is found worth retaining when tale, ballad, jest, or myth is transmitted by word of mouth or on the written page from generation to generation or from land to land" (19). The point here is that these motifs occur in a tradition of folk literature of which fairy tale is a part.

2. Although Campbell maintains that the hero journey is the monomyth, fairy tale incorporates several other "types" in addition to this one. Examples are: Type 300, The dragon-slayer; Type M1.7010, Revenge for being teased.

3. Interestingly, the narrative line of an Indian legend is a male's journey to the land of the grandfather.

4. Rosowski points out that the distinction between "featureless" (*Archbishop* 17) and "crowded with features all exactly alike" is meaningless (165). Thus the analogy between the prairies and the "desert of ovens" is fitting.

5. Sharon O'Brien discusses Cather's use of enclosed and open spaces and their significance in her chapter "Disclosure and Concealment: The First Stories" (195).

6. The roots of this tale are ancient, and versions of this story are found in many cultures. An Austrian version is called "The Gentleman Made of Groats." *Frankenstein, Pygmalion,* and *Pinocchio* are descended from this tale. Gingerbread is itself a fairy tale motif; for example, the witch's house in "Hansel and Gretel" is made of gingerbread.

7. Roskowski says that "Jim Burden saw Ántonia conventionally as his 'Snow White,' retreated when she contradicted that ideal, then returned to reaffirm her as a New World Earth Mother" (12). Thus he exchanges one image of permanence for another.

8. It is interesting, too, to note Cather's use of imagery of permanence in *Alexander's Bridge,* in which Bartley Alexander tries to hold onto his youth.

9. Cather also alludes to a place such as this in *Alexander's Bridge*. Alexander is traveling by train to his death; from the window he sees a group of boys sitting around a campfire on the edge of a marsh. The scene takes "his mind back a long way, to a campfire on a sandbar in a Western river, and he wished he could go back and sit down with them. He could remember exactly how the world had looked then" (116).

10. We should note here that Jim is yet another of Cather's fifteen-year-olds, fairy tale's favorite age for a person on the threshold of adulthood. Also, Ántonia "was a tall, strong young girl, although her *fifteenth* [my emphasis] birthday had just slipped by" (122) when Jim first sees her plowing and notices she is no longer a little girl.

11. Cather makes significant use of *Die Walküre* in her early short story "The Garden Lodge," as well as in *The Song of the Lark.*

12. According to Schrach, Cather's other possible sources for the wolf story are Browning's "Ivan Ivanovitch" and *Shukar Balan: The White Lamb,* by Mela Meisner Lindsay.

13. One questions here how the pattern is interpreted for a female.

14. These motifs are all classified numerically in Stith Thompson's index.

Chapter 3

1. In Perrault's tale, there are seven good fairies and one old fairy; thus she is not the *thirteenth,* but the *eighth.* This is a good example of how the tales were changed, and with them their interpretations.

2. O'Brien argues that one of Cather's profoundest fears was that of being silenced, that she was "preoccupied with the mother's power to reduce a child—a potential artist—to silence, the subtext of the Nebraska stories" (207). In fairy tale the princess is silent—in fact, all good women are usually silent in fairy tale.

3. Max Lüthi's article on Shakespeare shows "how a great artist can recapture the folk-tale power we no longer have" (*LO* 8). It is available in German: "Gründe der Faszinationskraft Shakespeares." Lüthi applies the polar contrast of folk tale to Shakespeare.

4. Yet another of Cather's fairy-tale princesses is Gabrielle Longstreet in "The Old Beauty."

5. These objects can be read as genital symbols, implying that Myra is relying entirely on sex.

Chapter 4

1. In *My Ántonia,* Jim Burden's tutor at the university is "the brilliant and inspiring young scholar" (257) Gaston *Cleric* [my emphasis], head of the Latin department, who has been "enfeebled by a long illness in Italy" [my emphasis] (257). Jim says that Cleric "introduced him to the world of ideas" (258).

2. The "simple" priest here gets the better of his wealthy patron by con man tactics repeatedly used for amusement in frontier humor tales.

3. *The Golden Legend,* as well as Puvis de Chavannes, was clearly in Cather's mind when she wrote *Archbishop* and her next novel, *Shadows on the Rock;* these works apply to both novels.

4. Readers have been puzzled by the lost El Greco painting of St. Francis, mentioned in the prologue, which never turns up again in the novel. Perhaps the Archbishop himself comes to represent this lost work of art. Latour is as out of place in the American West as the painting, but he learns to adapt and even to belong. Cather's point here might be that great art from the civilized world is transplanted to America, takes root, and comes alive in a transformed state. The images of Latour in his garden, where he spends his best years, recall those of St. Francis, who is usually pictured in a garden.

5. New Mexico itself is synonymous with the fairy-tale forest in which the heroes forge a new identity.

6. Cather employs this motif in *My Ántonia,* where Mr. Shimerda kneels and prays under the Burden's Christmas tree.

7. O'Brien's theory is that this search for the mother is the underlying motif in Cather's fiction, as well as in her life.

Chapter 5

1. Cather's relationship to the Menuhin children is explored by Robert Magidoff in *Yehudi Menuhin: The Story of the Man and the Musician* (Garden City, N.Y.: Doubleday, 1955).

2. Bettelheim asserts that the fear of being deserted is not restricted to any particular period of development, but that it occurs at all ages in the unconscious. He says that "the older person might find it considerably more difficult to admit consciously his fear of being deserted by his parents . . . and this is even more reason to let the fairy tale speak to his unconscious, give body to his unconscious anxieties, and relieve them, without this ever coming to conscious awareness" (15).

3. Cather's impulse to write a fairy tale is explained to some extent by Mircea Eliade: Fairy tales "are the expression of a psychodrama that answers a deep need in the human being. Every man wants to experience certain perilous situations, to confront exceptional ordeals, to make his way into the Other World—and he experiences all this, on the level of his imaginative life, by hearing or reading fairy tales" (as quoted by Bethelheim, 35).

Bibliography

A. Works by Willa Cather

April Twilights (1903); poems. Edited with an intro. by Bernice Slote. Lincoln: Univ. of Nebraska Press, 1962.

The Troll Garden. New York: McClure, Phillips, 1905.

Alexander's Bridge. New York: A. A. Knopf, 1912.

O Pioneers! Boston: Houghton Mifflin, 1913.

The Song of the Lark. Boston: Houghton Mifflin, 1915.

My Ántonia. New ed. Boston: Houghton Mifflin, 1918.

One of Ours. New York: A. A. Knopf, 1922.

A Lost Lady. New York: A. A. Knopf, 1923.

The Professor's House. New York: A. A. Knopf, 1925.

My Mortal Enemy. New York: A. A. Knopf, 1926.

Death Comes for the Archbishop. New York: A. A. Knopf, 1927.

Shadows on the Rock. New York: A. A. Knopf, 1931.

Obscure Destinies. New York: A. A. Knopf, 1932.

Lucy Gayheart. New York: A. A. Knopf, 1935.

Not Under Forty. New York: A. A. Knopf, 1936.

Sapphira and the Slave Girl. New York: A. A. Knopf, 1940.

The Old Beauty and Others. New York: A. A. Knopf, 1948.

On Writing. 1st ed. Critical studies on writing as an art, with a foreword by Stephen Tennant. New York: A. A. Knopf, 1949.

The Troll Garden. With an afterword by Katherine Anne Porter. New York: New American Library, 1961.

Willa Cather's Collected Short Fiction, 1892–1912. Virginia Faulkner, ed. Introduction by Mildred R. Bennett. Lincoln: Univ. of Nebraska Press, 1965.

The Kingdom of Art. Selected and edited with two essays and a commentary by Bernice Slote. Lincoln: Univ. of Nebraska Press, 1966.

The World and the Parish. Willa Cather's articles and reviews, 1983–1902. Selected and edited with a commentary by William M. Curtin. Lincoln: Univ. of Nebraska Press, 1970.

Uncle Valentine and Other Stories. Willa Cather's uncollected short fiction, 1915–1929. Edited with an introduction by Bernice Slote. Lincoln: Univ. of Nebraska Press, 1973.

B. Works about Willa Cather

Bennett, Mildred R. *The World of Willa Cather*. Lincoln: Univ. of Nebraska Press, 1961.

————. "A Note on the White Bear Stories." *Willa Cather Pioneer Memorial Newsletter* 17 (Summer 1973).

————. "Willa Cather and the Prairie." *Nebraska History* 56 (1975): 231–35.

————. "The Childhood Worlds of Willa Cather." *Great Plains Quarterly* 2, no. 4 (Fall 1982): 204–9.

Bloom, Edward A. and Lillian D. *Willa Cather's Gift of Sympathy* with a pref. by Harry T. Moore. Carbondale: Southern Illinois Univ. Press, 1962.

Bogan, Louise. "American Classic." *New Yorker* 7 (8 August 1931): 19–22.

Borgman, Paul. "The Dialectic of Willa Cather's Moral Vision." *Ranascence* 27 (1976): 145–59.

Brown, E. K. *Willa Cather, a Critical Biography*. New York: A. A. Knopf, 1953.

Brown, Ruth, and Ruth Crone. *Only One Point of the Compass: Willa Cather in the Northeast*. Danbury, Conn.: Archer Editions, 1980.

Butcher, Fanny. *Many Lives, Many Loves*. New York: Harper & Row, 1972.

Cassai, Mary Ann. "Symbolic Techniques in Selected Novels of Willa Cather." DAI 39:2269A-70A.

Crone, Ruth, and Marion Brown. *Willa Cather: The Woman and Her Works*. New York: Scribner, 1970.

Daiches, David. *Willa Cather, A Critical Introduction*. Ithaca, N.Y.: Cornell Univ. Press, 1951.

Edel, Leon. *Willa Cather, The Paradox of Success*. A lecture delivered in 1959. Washington Reference Dept., Library of Congress, 1960.

Fryer, Judith. *Felicitous Space: The Imaginative Structures of Edith Wharton and Willa Cather*. Chapel Hill: Univ. of N. Carolina Press, 1986.

Gerber, Philip L. *Willa Cather*. Boston: Twayne, 1975.

Hiers, John T. and Floyd C. Watkins. "A Chat with Willa Cather." *Resources for American Literary Study* (Spring 1979): 35–38. [Includes text of 1921 interview, 36–38.]

Knopf, A. A. *Willa Cather*. A biographical sketch, an English opinion, reviews and articles concerning her later books, and an abridged biblio. Folcroft, Pa.: Folcroft Library Editions, 1975.

Lathrop, JoAnna. *Willa Cather: A Checklist of Her Published Writing*. Lincoln: Univ. of Nebraska Press, 1975.

Lewis, Edith. *Willa Cather Living*. A personal record. [1st. ed.] New York: A. A. Knopf, 1953.

Magidoff, Robert. *Yehudi Menuhin: The Story of the Man and the Musician*. Garden City, N.Y.: Doubleday, 1955.

Massey, David G. "Simplicity and Suggestiveness in Willa Cather's Revised and Republished Fiction." DAI 40:2063A, 1978.

McFarland, Dorothy Tuck. *Willa Cather*. New York: Frederick Ungar, 1972.

Moers, Ellen. *Literary Women*. Garden City, N.Y.: Doubleday, 1976.

Mosely, Ann. *Voyage Perilous: Willa Cather's Mythic Quest*. Ann Arbor, Mich.: University Microfilms, 1974.

Murphy, John J., ed. *Five Essays on Willa Cather: The Merrimack Symposium*. North Andover, Mass.: Merrimack College, 1974.

————, ed. *Critical Essays on Willa Cather*. Boston: G. K. Hall, 1984.

O'Brien, Sharon. *Willa Cather: The Emerging Voice*. New York: Oxford Univ. Press, 1987.

O'Connor, Margaret. "A Guide to the Letters of Willa Cather." *Resources for American Literary Study* 4 (1974): 145–72.

Pers, Mona. *Willa Cather's Children*. Diss. Uppsala Univ., Sweden, 1975. Stockholm, Sweden: Almqvist and Wiksell Intl., distributor.

Randall, John H. *The Landscape and the Looking Glass: Willa Cather's Search for Value*. Westport, Conn.: Greenwood Press, 1973 [1960].

Robinson, Phyllis C. *Willa: The Life of Willa Cather*. Garden City, N.Y.: Doubleday, 1983.

Romines, Marjorie Ann. "House, Procession, River: Domestic Ritual in the Fiction of Seven American Women, 1877–1972." DAI 38:5467A, 1978.

Rose, Phyllis, *Writing of Women*. Middletown, Conn.: Wesleyan Univ. Press, 1985.

Rosowski, Susan J. *The Voyage Perilous: Willa Cather's Romanticism*. Lincoln, Nebraska: Univ. of Nebraska Press, 1886.

Sacken, Jeannee P. *"A Certain Slant of Light": Aesthetics of First-Person Narration in Gide and Cather*. New York: Garland, 1985.

Schrach, Paul. "Russian Wolves in Folktales and Literature of the Plains: A Question of Origins." *Great Plains Quarterly* 3, no. 2 (1983): 67–78.

Schroeter, James M., ed. *Willa Cather and Her Critics*. Ithaca, N.Y.: Cornell Univ. Press, 1967.

Schwind, Jean Denise. "Pictorial Art in Willa Cather's Fiction." DAI 44:3687A, 1984.

Sergeant, Elizabeth Shepley. *Willa Cather: A Memoir*. Lincoln: Univ. of Nebraska Press, 1963.

Skaggs, Merrill M. *"Death Comes for the Archbishop:* Cather's Mystery and Manners." *American Literature* 57, no. 3 (1985): 395–406.

———. "A Good Girl in Her Place: Cather's *Shadows on the Rock*." *Religion and Literature* 17, no. 3 (Autumn 1985): 27–36.

Slote, Bernice. "Willa Cather: Storyteller for Children." *Willa Cather Pioneer Memorial Newsletter* 17, no. 3 (Summer 1973): 1–2.

———. *Sixteen Modern American Authors*. Durham: Duke Univ. Press, 1974.

———. "An Exploration of Cather's Early Writing." *Great Plains Quarterly* 2, no. 4 (1982): 210–17.

Slote, Bernice, and Virginia Faulkner, eds. *The Art of Willa Cather*. Lincoln: Univ. of Nebraska Press, 1974.

Stouck, David. *Willa Cather's Imagination*. Lincoln: Univ. of Nebraska Press, 1975.

———. "Women Writers in the Mainstream: A Review Essay." *Texas Studies in Literature and Language* 20 (1979): 660–70.

Sutherland, Donald. "Willa Cather: The Classic Voice." In *The Art of Willa Cather*, B. Slote and V. Faulkner, eds. 1975. 156–82, 263.

Trilling, Lionel. "Willa Cather." In *Speaking of Literature and Society*. Ed. Diana Trilling. New York: Harcourt Brace Jovanovich, 1980.

Van Ghent, Dorothy. "Willa Cather." In *Seven American Women Writers of the Twentieth Century*. Ann Arbor: Univ. of Michigan Press, 1977.

Welty, Eudora. "Willa Cather: American Experience and European Tradition." In *The Art of Willa Cather*, B. Slote and V. Faulkner, eds. 1975. 43–64, 260.

Woodress, James L. *Willa Cather: Her Life and Art*. Lincoln: Univ. of Nebraska Press, 1975.

Woods, Lucia. *Willa Cather: A Pictorial Memoir*. Photos. Text by Bernice Slote. Lincoln: Univ. of Nebraska Press, 1973.

Yongue, Patricia Lee. "Willa Cather's Aristocrats." *Southern Humanities Review* 14 (1980): 43–56, 111–125.

C. Works on Folklore and General Topics

Aarne, Antti A. *The Types of the Folktale*. Helsinki: Suomalainen Tiedeakatemia, 1961.

Andersen, Hans Christian. *Eighty Fairy Tales*. New York: Pantheon, 1976.

Bates, Katherine Lee, ed. *Norse Stories*. New York: Rand McNally, 1902.

Bettelheim, Bruno. *Symbolic Wounds*. Glencoe: The Free Press, 1954.

———. *The Uses of Enchantment: The Meaning and Importance of Fairy Tales*. New York: A. A. Knopf, 1975.

Biard, Jean Dominique. *The Style of La Fontaine's Fables*. New York: Barnes and Noble, 1966.

Briggs, Katherine M. *A Dictionary of British Folk Tales*. 4 vols. Bloomington: Indiana Univ. Press, 1970.

———. *An Encyclopedia of Fairies*. New York: Pantheon Books, 1976.

Burton, Richard. *The Arabian Nights' Entertainments*. 13 vols. London: H. S. Nichols, 1894–97.

Campbell, Joseph. *The Hero with a Thousand Faces*. New York: Pantheon Books, 1953.

Cox, Marian Roalfe. *Cinderella: Three Hundred and Forty-five Variants*. London: The Folk-Lore Society, David Nutt, 1893.

Danner, Richard. *Patterns of Irony in the Fables of La Fontaine*. Athens: Ohio Univ. Press, 1985.

Dorson, Richard M. *Folklore: Selected Essays*. Bloomington: Indiana Univ. Press, 1972.

Dundes, Alan. *Interpreting Folklore*. Bloomington: Indiana Univ. Press, 1980.

———. *Cinderella: A Folklore Casebook*. New York: Garland, 1982.

Edmunds, Lowell, and Alan Dundes. *Oedipus: A Folklore Casebook*. New York: Garland, 1984.

Erikson, Erik H. *Identity, Youth and Crisis*. New York: Norton, 1968.

Fromm, Erich. *The Forgotten Language*. New York: Rinehart, 1951.

Frye, Northrup. *Fables of Identity: Studies in Poetic Mythology*. New York: Harcourt, Brace & World, 1963.

Funk and Wagnalls Dictionary of Folklore. 2 vols. New York: Funk and Wagnalls, 1950.

Gilbert, Sandra M., and Susan Gubar. *The Madwoman in the Attic: The Woman Writer and the Nineteenth Century Literary Imagination*. New Haven: Yale Univ. Press, 1979.

Grimm, Jacob. *Teutonic Mythology*. 4 vols. Trans. from 4th ed. by James Steven Stallybrass. London: George Bell and Sons, 1883.

Grimm, Jacob and Wilhelm K. Grimm. *Grimm's Fairy Tales*. New York: Pantheon Books, 1944.

———. *The Grimm's German Folk Tales*. Carbondale, Ill.: Southern Illinois Univ. Press, 1960.

Guiton, Margaret. *La Fontaine: Poet and Counterpoet*. New Brunswick, N.J.: Rutgers Univ. Press, 1961.

Heuscher, Julius E. *A Psychiatric Study of Fairy Tales*. Springfield: Charles Thomas, 1963.

Hume, Kathryn. *Fantasy and Mimesis: Responses to Reality in Western Literature*. London: Methuen, 1984.

Jacobs, Joseph. *English Fairy Tales*. London: David Nutt, 1890.

———. *More English Tales*. London: David Nutt, 1895.

Journal of American Folklore. American Folklore Society, Boston, 1888ff.

Kolbenschlags, Madonna. *Kiss Sleeping Beauty Good-bye: Breaking the Spell of Feminine Myths and Models*. New York: Bantam, 1981.

Lang, Andrew, ed. *The Fairy Books*. 12 vols. London: Longmans, Green and Co., 1889ff.

———, ed. *Perrault's Popular Tales*. Oxford: Clarendon Press, 1988.

Lederer, Wolfgang. *The Kiss of the Snow Queen: Hans Christian Andersen and Man's Redemption by Woman*. Berkeley: Univ. of California Press, 1986.

Lüthi, Max. *The Fairytale as Art Form and Portrait of Man*. Trans. Jon Erickson, Bloomington: Indiana Univ. Press, 1984.

———. *Once Upon a Time: On the Nature of Fairy Tales*. Trans. Lee Chadeayne and Paul Gottwald. Bloomington: Indiana Univ. Press, 1984.

Miller, Alice. *Thou Shalt Not Be Aware: Society's Betrayal of the Child*. New York: Farrar, Straus & Giroux, 1984.

Neumann, Erich. *The Great Mother: An Analysis of the Archetype*. Trans. Ralph Manheim. New York: Pantheon Books, 1955.

Opie, Iona and Peter. *The Classic Fairy Tales*. London: Oxford Univ. Press.

Perrault, Charles. *Histoires ou Contes du Temps Passé*. Paris, 1697.

Phelps, Ethel Johnston. *The Maid of the North*. New York: Holt, Rinehart and Winston, 1981.

Piaget, Jean. *The Child's Concept of the World*. New York: Harcourt Brace, 1929.

Propp, Vladimir. *Morphology of the Folktale*. 2nd ed., rev. and ed. Louis A. Wagner. New intro. Alan Dundes. London: Austin, 1968.

Rubenstein, B. "The Meaning of the Cinderella Story in the Development of a Little Girl." *American Imago* 12 (1955), 197–205.

Saintyves, Paul. *Les Contes de Perrault et les Recits Parallèles*. Paris: E. Nourry, 1923.

Schwab, Gustav. *Gods and Heroes: Myths and Epics of Ancient Greece*. New York: Pantheon Books, 1946.

Sexton, Anne. *Transformations*. Boston: Houghton Mifflin, 1971.

Soriano, Marc. *Les Contes de Perrault*. Paris: Gallimard, 1968.

Spink, Reginald. *Hans Christian Andersen: The Man and His Work*. Copenhagen: Host and Sons, 1972.

Tatar, Maria. *The Hard Facts of the Grimms' Fairy Tales*. Princeton: Princeton Univ. Press, 1987.

Thompson, Stith. *The Folk Tale*. New York: Dryden Press, 1946.

———. *Motif Index of Folk Literature*. 6 vols. Bloomington: Indiana Univ. Press, 1984.

———, ed. *One Hundred Favorite Folktales*. Bloomington: Indiana Univ. Press, 1984.

de Voragine, Jacobus. *The Golden Legend*. Trans. and adapted from the Latin by Granger Ryan and Helmut Repperger. New York: Longmans, Green and Co., 1941.

von Franz, Marie Louise. *Interpretation of Fairy Tales*. New York: Spring Publications, 1970.

Waelti-Walters, Jennifer. *Fairy Tales and the Female Imagination*. Montreal: Eden Press, 1892.

Walker, Barbara G. *The Woman's Encyclopedia of Myths and Secrets*. San Francisco: Harper & Row, 1983.

———. *The Tarot*. San Francisco: Harper & Row, 1986.

Whitman, Edward C. *The Symbolic Quest*. Princeton: Princeton Univ. Press, 1969.

Zipes, Jack. *Breaking the Magic Spell: Radical Theories of Folk and Fairy Tales*. New York: Methuen, 1979.

———. *Fairy Tales and the Art of Subversion*. London: Heinemann Educational Books, 1983.

———. *Don't Bet on the Prince: Contemporary Feminist Fairy Tales in North America and England*. New York: Methuen, 1986.

Index